214

SONGS THAT LIFT THE HEART

SONGS THAT LIFT THE HEART

A Personal Story by
GEORGE BEVERLY SHEA
with Fred Bauer

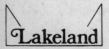

Scripture references in this volume are from the *Authorised Version of the Bible*.

Grateful acknowledgment is extended to those who made it possible to include the music and words of the hymns in this volume.

Used by permission of the Chancel Music Company: "Adoration" by Mrs. A. J. Shea, copyright 1947 by George Beverly Shea, © 1965 by Chancel Music Co.; "Blue Galilee" by George Beverly Shea, copyright 1947 by George Beverly Shea, assigned to Chancel Music Inc., International copyright secured; "I'd Rather Have Jesus" by Rhea F. Miller and George Beverly Shea, copyright 1922 Rhea F. Miller, copyright renewal 1950, copyright 1939 George Beverly Shea, renewal 1966, assigned to Chancel Music Inc., international copyright secured (BMI); "Let Not Your Heart Be Troubled" by Arthur Smith and George Beverly Shea, © copyright 1970 by Chancel Music Inc.; "Songs in the Night" by J. Thurston Noé and Dr. Will Houghton, © copyright assigned to Chancel Music, Inc.

"The Wonder of It All" by George Beverly Shea © 1956 by Chancel Music, Inc. International copyright secured.

Used by permission of Fiesta Music Inc.: "I Found What I Wanted" by Ralph Carmichael.

Used by permission of Hope Publishing Company: "Singing I Go" by E. E. Hewitt and William J. Kirkpatrick; "Have Thine Own Way" by Adelaide A. Pollard and George Stebbins; "The Christ of Every Road" by Dr. Will Houghton and Wendell P. Loveless; "Songs in the Night" by Wendell P. Loveless; "He Will Hold Me Fast" by Ada R. Habershon and Robert Harkness.

Used by permission of the Lynn Music Corporation: "Acres of Diamonds" by Arthur Smith and Robert Harkness. © Copyright 1959 by Lynn Music Corp., P.O. Box 153, Brewster, N.Y. International Copyright Secured. All Rights Reserved.

Used by permission of the Rodeheaver Co.: "The Old Rugged Cross" by George Bennard, Copyright 1913 by George Bennard. The Rodeheaver Co., Owner. Renewed 1941 (extended); "Then Jesus Came" by Oswald J. Smith and Homer Rodeheaver, Copyright 1940 by the Rodeheaver Co. © Renewed 1968.

All Rights Reserved; "Beyond the Sunset" by Virgil and Blanche Brock, Copyright 1936 by the Rodeheaver Co. © Renewed 1964. All Rights Reserved; "Speak My Lord" by George Bennard. Copyright 1911 by George Bennard. Renewed 1939 (extended), by George Bennard. Assigned to the Rodeheaver Co.

Used by permission of G. Schirmer, Inc.: "Thou Light of Light" by J. Thurstin Noe, Copyright 1958 by G. Schirmer, Inc.

The quoted material from *Streams in the Desert* by Mrs. Charles E. Cowman is copyrighted by Cowman Publications, Inc. of Grand Rapids, Michigan, and is used by permission of Zondervan Publishing House.

The article by Glenn D. Kittler from *Guideposts*, © 1964 Guideposts Associated, Carmel, N.Y. is used by permission.

Reminiscences and Gospel Hymn Stories by George Stebbins, Copyright 1924, George H. Doran Company. Used by permission of Doubleday and Co., Inc.

Used by permission of the Malvern Music Company: "If You Know the Lord" by Bickley Reichner. Copyright 1951 Malvern Music Company.

Used by permission of Manna Music Inc.: "How Great Thou Art" by Carl Boberg, translated by Stuart K. Hine, © Copyright 1955 by Manna Music Inc., North Hollywood, California. International Copyright Secured. All Rights Reserved.

Used by permission of the Nazarene Publishing House: "The Love of God" by F. M. Lehman. Copyright 1917 and 1945 by Nazarene Publishing House.

Used by permission of Carlin Music Corporation: "It Took a Miracle" by John Peterson, Copyright 1948 by Percy B. Crawford. Copyright assigned to Hill and Range Songs, Inc.; "Oh, How Sweet It Is to Know" by Cindy Walker, Copyright © 1955 by Hill and Range Songs, Inc.

Contents

To people
everywhere who love
to tell that Old, Old
Story through song.

Foreword

One of the requisites for working on a book with George Beverly Shea is a sturdy suitcase. The reason is that this twenty-five-year veteran of Billy Graham Crusades is a man in perpetual motion. When we collaborated on *Then Sings My Soul,* his autobiography, I followed him from his headquarters just outside of Chicago ("Just a stone's throw from my second home, Chicago's O'Hare Airport," he jokes), to San Juan, Puerto Rico, to New York, to West Palm Beach, Florida, back to the Shea home and finally East where we spent three days together in my home in Princeton, New Jersey, and another marathon day in a New York City hotel room, checking galley proofs just before the book went off to press — and just before my peripatetic friend went off on another singing mission.

The preparation of this book has required no less traveling on my part, though it has been limited primarily to excursions between New York and Chicago. One trip to Nashville to meet Bev and another with him to Ottawa, Canada, were exceptions. (On my way home from Canada, I visited Bev's ninety-year-old mother in Syracuse.) I did consider trailing Bev to the Holy Land, Rome, and Australia in the spring, but a look at his jam-packed schedule convinced me we would make little progress on the manuscript, so I stayed behind compiling and weaving together the material that we already had agreed should be included. Questions that I had or new thoughts, additions, or corrections from him were passed back and forth in the mails.

To paraphrase a popular TV commercial, someone might ask: Is this any way to write a book? My response would be: With George Beverly Shea, it is the only way. Waiting for him to come stationary, sit down to a typewriter and pore over it for the months it takes to prepare a manuscript, would simply mean that a book would not be forthcoming. Therefore, we have worked out an alternative, a catch-as-catch-can procedure which in at least one previous effort produced favorable enough results that we were encouraged to try again.

There was one junket which I should like to elaborate upon. That was to Nashville in February where I sat in on the recording of Bev's thirty-sixth RCA album, *Amazing Grace*. I must tell you about this experience, for it is fresh in mind and will serve as well as anything to paint the personality of this much-admired man. Traveling about with him, being with him on the platform, associating with his friends on the Billy Graham team, coming to know his lovely wife, Erma, and his fine son and daughter, Ron and Lainie, corresponding with him, sharing some of his joys and disappointments, watching and listening to the people who have been blessed by his singing, I have come to understand the veneration people all over the world have for him. He is worthy of it, but I might add—unaffected by it.

Without doubt, he is one of the most humble men I've ever been around. People who have known Bev from "the early days" say he is still the same fellow who unassumingly and somewhat shyly played the organ in his father's church; the same young man who worked in a New York life insurance company and sang on the side; the same modest announcer who worked for a Chicago radio station; the same quiet, dignified gospel hymn singer Billy Graham sought out when he began his world-wide ministry.

But most of the people I've mentioned are of a religious persuasion and most of the settings of a spiritual tone. I wondered as I flew into Nashville, considered by many to be the music capital of the country, how Bev would respond to a more secular milieu, how he would be accepted in an arena where the purveyors of musical talent often talk in terms of top billing, top forty, Gold records, showmanship, color, marketability—terms many would consider incongruous with sacred music.

I should not have been surprised to find Bev the same as always. The people around him—top names in popular music, but not necessarily strangers to gospel music—greeted him with genuine warmth and affection. Bev's admiration for people such as his producer, Danny Davis (of Nashville Brass fame); for his arranger-director Bill Walker who took a bow every week on the Johnny Cash TV show; for the former Anita Kerr quartet (now the Nashville Sounds) who gave him vocal backing; for the eighteen-piece orchestra; for the recording technicians—was only surpassed by their obvious admiration for him and his professionalism.

Professionalism is the right word. Painstakingly, I watched this assembled team rehearse until they felt they were ready to cut a selection. Then, I listened carefully to what my untrained ear thought was a perfect rendition—only to see the entire number repeated again and again until everyone was satisfied. The demands Bev makes on himself—the perfection upon which he insists—was particularly revealing. No wonder his standing among professional artists is so high. No wonder he has been nominated for a "Grammy" award (the recording industry's equivalent of an Oscar) every year since 1963. (He won in 1966 with an album entitled *Southland Favorites*.)

I particularly enjoyed a fast-moving arrangement of "Do, Lord," a song I remember singing as a boy at a church camp, near St. Mary's, Ohio:

> **I've got a home in glory land that outshines the sun,**
> **I've got a home in glory land that outshines the sun,**
> **I've got a home in glory land that outshines the sun,**
> **Way beyond the blue.**
>
> *Do, Lord, oh do, Lord, oh do remember me,*
> *Do, Lord, oh do, Lord, oh do remember me,*
> *Do, Lord, oh do, Lord, oh do remember me,*
> *Way beyond the blue.*

9

What fun the band, the group and Bev all had tapping their feet and clapping hands as they sang this happy tune!

Balancing this rouser was the beautiful title selection for the album, the Judy Collins-revived revival classic, *Amazing Grace*. Introducing it, Bev recalled briefly at the outset the time he visited the grave of John Newton, its composer, in an Olney, England, churchyard, a short distance from the pulpit Newton once filled. Bev quoted the words inscribed on that headstone:

JOHN NEWTON, CLERK, ONCE AN INFIDEL AND LIBERTINE, A SERVANT OF SLAVES IN AFRICA, WAS BY THE RICH MERCY OF OUR LORD AND SAVIOUR JESUS CHRIST PRESERVED, RESTORED, PARDONED, AND APPOINTED TO PREACH THE FAITH HE HAD LONG LABORED TO DESTROY.

Then, he sang that old hymn:

> Amazing grace! how sweet the sound,
> That saved a wretch like me!
> I once was lost, but now am found,
> Was blind, but now I see.

When he had finished, the engineer's room outside the studio was nearly full of visitors and employees who had filed in to hear in detail the haunting lyrics and music that had filtered magnetically through the halls and offices of that famous recording studio. Not a few in the audience were watery-eyed as they walked away.

That's the moving effect Bev Shea has on people everywhere when he sings sacred music. Billy Graham has observed, "More than any other singer in modern times, Bev literally sings the message of Jesus Christ to the hearts of people."

In this book, George Beverly Shea talks about the music he loves, naming his favorite gospel songs and telling many warm, personal anecdotes about them that reveal why they mean so much to him. After reading the pages that follow I think you'll have an even greater appreciation for the man and his music.

FRED BAUER

10

Introduction

What makes a good hymn? A lasting hymn? One that catches on and stands the test of time?

I have often asked myself these questions as I select music for a Crusade, for a concert, for a record album, and I've never been able to see clearly why one song gains favor and another with apparently equal technical quality passes quickly from the scene. Others who are much more knowledgeable on the subject of sacred music than I have confessed equal bafflement. My conclusion is that gospel hymns which gain a kind of immortality have some special heart-touching quality, a spiritual depth and sincerity that surpasses others. Often they are rather simple melodies with simple messages and rather obvious end rhymes, but they touch people where they live; they move them, change them, inspire them.

Sometimes I find clues in the story behind a gospel hymn (not, however, that every "classic" in this special musical category has some dramatic story related to its writing). To the contrary, the lyrics for a good many of your favorites and mine were written by people who "just wrote poetry every day." And the melodies were composed by skilled craftsmen in this trade. But it must be added that many hymns do have a fascinating origin, like *Amazing Grace,* of which Fred Bauer has already spoken. It helps me to interpret the words when I know that John Newton, the author, was the son of a sea captain, who, after his mother's death, joined his father at age eleven on his ship.

I'm interested to know that he and his father apparently had a generation gap and they came to a parting of the ways, and that John's life turned into one of degradation—fighting, drinking, jail. Serving on a slave ship, he so infuriated the captain that he was made a slave of the slaves—another chapter in the Prodigal Son story. But then, somehow, John Newton came upon a copy of Thomas à Kempis' book, *Imitation of Christ,* and his heart responded. I can see him pondering those all-surrendering prayers of the author:

> O Lord, Thou knowest what is best for us; let this or that be done, as Thou shalt please. Give what Thou wilt, and how much Thou wilt, and when Thou wilt. Deal with me as Thou thinkest good, and as best pleaseth Thee: Set me where Thou wilt, and deal with me in all things as Thou wilt. Behold, I am Thy servant, prepared for all things; for I desire not to live unto myself, but unto Thee; and oh that I could do it worthily and perfectly!

But it took a storm at sea in which Newton almost lost his life for him to turn everything over to God. He became a minister at age thirty-nine and during his fifteen-year pastorate at Olney, England, he wrote the words to many hymns. The great composer William Cowper, also of Olney, set many of them to music and they collaborated on a famous hymnal. So with that background, I know what Newton is talking about when he writes about an amazing grace:

> **That saved a wretch like me!**
> **I once was lost, but now am found,**
> **Was blind, but now I see.**

I noted a few years ago that when *Christian Herald* magazine polled its readers, "Amazing Grace" was ninth on their all-time favorite list. A look at the results of that tally conducted by *Christian Herald* is most revealing:

THE FAVORITE FIFTY

1 The Old Rugged Cross
2 What A Friend We Have in Jesus
3 In the Garden
4 How Great Thou Art!
5 Sweet Hour of Prayer
6 Abide With Me
7 Rock of Ages
8 Nearer, My God, to Thee
9 Amazing Grace
10 Jesus, Lover of My Soul
11 Beyond the Sunset
12 Blessed Assurance
13 Lead, Kindly Light
14 My Faith Looks Up to Thee
15 Jesus, Savior, Pilot Me
16 Faith of Our Fathers
17 I Need Thee Every Hour
18 Have Thine Own Way
19 God Will Take Care of You
20 I Love to Tell the Story
21 Just As I Am
22 A Mighty Fortress
23 How Firm a Foundation
24 Ivory Palaces
25 Take Time to Be Holy
26 Holy, Holy, Holy
27 Whispering Hope
28 Onward, Christian Soldiers
29 Dear Lord and Father of Mankind
30 This Is My Father's World
31 When I Survey the Wondrous Cross
32 Fairest Lord Jesus
33 The Church's One Foundation
34 Just a Closer Walk With Thee
35 Great Is Thy Faithfulness
36 The Love of God
37 Beautiful Garden of Prayer
38 Near the Cross
39 An Evening Prayer
40 Be Still, My Soul
41 Blest Be the Tie That Binds
42 O Love That Wilt Not Let Me Go
43 O Master, Let Me Walk With Thee
44 In the Sweet By and By
45 Are Ye Able?
46 Living for Jesus
47 He Leadeth Me
48 Love Divine, All Love Excelling
49 When the Roll Is Called Up Yonder
50 Near to the Heart of God

Like favorite Scripture verses, favorite songs have a way of undergirding us when "the way grows drear." Not long ago, I read a fascinating account of the *Pueblo* crew (*My Anchor Held**

* Lakeland No. 213

by Stephen Harris), captured by the North Koreans and imprisoned for eleven months. I read with great excitement the section which told about the men compiling a "Bible" from memory. Various ones contributed remembered verses and copied them onto the scraps of paper available. Then, at great personal risk, they passed them among each other, drawing strength and courage from the Word of God.

The author of that book wrote, "I prayed for strength not to hate the *Korcoms* [the Korean Communists]. Scripture helped me. Fortunately, the chaplain friend who had shown me the way to Christ had recommended that I enroll in the Navigators' program of Scripture memory."

After reading that statement, I wondered what verses would sustain me if the freedom I take for granted living in the United States were ever withdrawn. What passages would help me uphold my faith? Surely, I would include:

- The Lord is my shepherd; I shall not want.
  He maketh me to lie down in green pastures: he leadeth me beside the still waters.
  He restoreth my soul: he leadeth me in the paths of righteousness for his name's sake.
  Yea, though I walk through the valley of the shadow of death, I will fear no evil: for thou art with me; thy rod and thy staff they comfort me.
  Thou preparest a table before me in the presence of mine enemies: thou anointest my head with oil; my cup runneth over.
  Surely goodness and mercy shall follow me all the days of my life: and I will dwell in the house of the Lord for ever. (Psalm 23)

- For God so loved the world that he gave his only begotten Son, that whosoever believeth in him should not perish, but have everlasting life. (John 3 : 16)

- In my Father's house are many mansions: if it were not so, I would have told you. I go to prepare a place for you. (John 14 : 2)

14

- Take therefore no thought for the morrow . . . (Matthew 6:34). Consider the lilies of the field, how they grow; they toil not, neither do they spin: And yet I say unto you, That even Solomon in all his glory was not arrayed like one of these. (vs. 28, 29)

And I'd have the verse that I use whenever someone asks me to sign my John Henry for them, the twenty-eighth chapter of Psalms, verse seven:

- The Lord is my strength and my shield; my heart trusted in him, and I am helped: therefore my heart greatly rejoiceth; and with my song will I praise him.

Yes, with my song I would praise Him. If I were denied my freedom and access to my Bible, I, like the *Pueblo* crew, would have to call on my memory and recite long-treasured verses, many of which I learned as a boy. But after I had exhausted that source, I'm sure I would turn to gospel music, the hymns. Which hymns? The ones which have touched my heart, inspired me, sustained me. My mail, hymn requests, and personal comments from Christian friends indicate that many of the songs I've included in this book are your favorites, too. I hope so.

To Him be the glory!

Psa 28:7

1

Songs I Grew Up On

My father, the Reverend A. J. Shea, and I were on an afternoon shopping trip for Mother, as I recall. When we came out of a store in Houghton, New York, where we had recently moved from Winchester, Ontario, we met a tall, elderly woman making her way slowly up the street. She was walking in that slow, mincing step older people sometimes do, cautious not to lose balance.

Dad tipped his hat and said good-day to her as we passed. She stopped and looked up to see who was speaking. Smiling sweetly, she returned his greeting.

"Do you know who that was, Son?" he asked me on up the way. I turned and watched as she continued her careful progress. Though a distinguished woman (whom I would now describe as looking a lot like Whistler's Mother) I had no idea who she was.

"That," said Dad, "was Mrs. Clara Tear Williams. She writes hymns." There was a near reverence in his voice, and though I was only eight years old, I was duly impressed. Already I was fascinated by music and anyone who was involved in it. Mother played the piano, Dad, the violin, and I was beginning to pick things out on the piano. I sometimes had trouble sitting through sermons on Sunday, or when we had evangelistic services nightly for extended periods, but I was never restless when it was time for the congregation to sing or when the choir or a soloist would present a special number. I liked the music part of a service best of all. Mother's carrot-on-the-stick was, "Be good now, Beverly, it won't be long before we'll sing."

When Dad and I got home that afternoon, I told Mother about meeting Mrs. Williams, the hymn writer. She smiled knowingly and nodded her head. Then, she went to the piano bench and found a hymnal that contained one of Clara Tear Williams' compositions.

She explained that Mrs. Williams—a Weslyan Methodist like us—had written the words, but that the music had been written by Ralph E. Hudson, an Ohio publisher who also was an evangelistic singer.

Placing the book on the music rack and sitting down to the piano, Mother began playing that song with me on the bench beside her. It was beautiful. Up until then, I guess I figured all the songs we sang in church were written and published by people who lived in far off places like New York. I couldn't get over the fact that we had a real live composer in our very own town.

A few years later, when I was in my teens and began to sing solos, I memorized the hymn that Mother played that day and sang it. It was entitled "Satisfied" or "All My Life Long." Maybe you've sung it:

> All my life long I had panted
> For a drink from some cool spring,
> That I hoped would quench the burning
> Of the thirst I felt within.
>
> Feeding on the husks around me
> Till my strength was almost gone,
> Longed my soul for something better,
> Only still to hunger on.
>
> Poor was I and sought for riches,
> Something that would satisfy
> But the dust that gathered round me
> Only mawked my soul's sad cry.
>
> *Hallelujah! I have found Him—*
> *Whom my soul so long has craved!*
> *Jesus satisfies my longings;*
> *Through His blood I now am saved.*

18

As I think back to that incident concerning Clara Tear Williams, I realize that from my earliest days I was encircled by music and by people who loved it. The gospel songs were ever being sung in our home.

My mother was the one who first brought music into my life. I suppose like many mothers she sang to me in the crib, repeating little nursery rhymes and children's Bible songs of the "Jesus Loves Me" variety, but the first song that really made an impression on me was Mother's wake-up theme song, her alarm clock tune, William Kirkpatrick's "Singing I Go." Every weekday morning she would wake the family by going to the piano, making a run down the keyboard, and then filling the house with her sweet soprano voice:

> Singing I go along life's road,
> Praising the Lord, praising the Lord,
> Singing I go along life's road,
> For Jesus has lifted my load.

It's a little painful as I write this to think I won't be hearing Mother sing it again. Last summer I received word that she was ill and I rushed to the hospital in Syracuse to see her. She'd undergone emergency surgery and despite her ninety years had weathered it well. However, complications arose, and it seemed to be God's will to take her home. With all of her children gathered around her (with the exception of Alton, a missionary in Africa) she passed away on September 1, 1971.

A number which has always had a warm spot in my heart because of its buoyant melody and positive, uplifting lyrics, it has been good to me over the years.

When I went to Chicago to work as an announcer for WMBI, the Moody Bible Institute radio station, I had a fifteen-minute program in the morning called "Hymns from the Chapel" and "Singing I Go" was my theme song. I got into the habit of taking the last note, "for Jesus has lifted my load" all the way down to E flat, slow *porto mento*. It drew quite a little attention, and I remember one woman writing to tell me that her children listened every morning to hear that low note, so I kept doing it.

Later I recorded the song for RCA and named an album after it, and I include it often when I sing sacred music concerts around the country. It serves as a good change of pace for more somber hymns. At these evening concerts, artists such as Tedd Smith, Don Hustad, or John Innes usually accompany me and also present some piano and/or organ selections.

One time in 1945, I remember Don and I were traveling with Bob Pierce doing a series of programs between Los Angeles and Seattle. At every concert along the way, I sang "Singing I Go." In each instance, I told the story of how Mother sang it each morning, and that it was she who taught it to me. Don Hustad heard the anecdote so many times, he knew my lines by heart. But at the end of the tour, I surprised him. After concluding on that low E flat at a program in Seattle, I turned to Don and said into the microphone, "But you know, Don, I don't recall that Mother taught me that note." He nearly fell off the piano bench, convulsed with laughter.

There is another incident I remember about that West Coast trip, too.

We often traveled by Greyhound bus, sometimes riding all night to our next stop, like the trip between Portland and Klamath Falls. Bob and Don didn't have any trouble sleeping that night I recall, but I did. Going over those mountains and around those sharp curves, I'd close my eyes for brief catnaps, but the fear that our driver would do the same kept me awake most of the time. When we arrived in the morning, I was so tired and wrinkled and hungry that all I could think about was a good meal, a shower, and some shut-eye, but the bright-eyed man who met us at the station had other plans.

"Boy, I was worried you wouldn't make it," he said, relieved. "We've arranged for you to sing on a radio program this morning and you're on the air in fifteen minutes."

Another early recollection of mine related to music happened when I was five years old. We were living in the Gladstone Street parsonage in Winchester, Ontario, at the time and our church, the Wesleyan Methodist, which Dad served for twenty years, was in the midst of evangelistic services.

One Saturday morning, about 10 A.M. the Reverend John Vennard, who was conducting the services, stopped by to discuss the music he intended to use in the next service.

Sitting down to our old Bell piano (a red mahogany instrument which had come from England about the time Mother and Dad were married, January 1, 1900, and has been in the family ever since), Mr. Vennard said, "Here are two new hymns that I like. They are both written by George Bennard, a minister who lives in Michigan. This one was just published last year [1913]." Then, he began to play and sing a hymn that was soon to sweep the world. Enraptured, I stood at the end of the piano and listened.

> **On a hill far away stood an old rugged cross,**
> **The emblem of suffering and shame;**
> **And I love that old cross where the dearest and best**
> **For a world of lost sinners was slain.**
>
> *So I'll cherish the old rugged cross*
> *Till my trophies at last I lay down;*
> *I will cling to the old rugged cross,*
> *And exchange it some day for a crown.*

After that he played and sang "Speak, My Lord," another beautiful hymn that was to receive great universal appreciation. I wonder how many times I have sung it since.

> *Speak, my Lord, speak, my Lord,*
> *Speak and I'll be quick to answer thee,*
> *Speak, my Lord, speak, my Lord,*
> *Speak and I will answer, answer Thee.*

I first met the composer of those two great hymns in the early 1940s at Winona Lake, Indiana, 110 miles from Chicago. I'd go there to do remote broadcasts for WMBI, and during the summers Mr. Bennard was often on hand. Though a preacher — and a good one — he would sometimes sing. His voice was not trained or out of the ordinary but he had great feeling and expression and could really put over any hymn. I remember how moved I was when for the first time I heard him sing his own "The Old Rugged Cross."

Like my awe at seeing a real live composer as a boy when Dad pointed out Clara Tear Williams, I remember how people would whisper to each other whenever they saw Mr. Bennard on the Winona Lake grounds, at the sweet shop or in the restaurant.

"He wrote the words to the 'Old Rugged Cross,' " mothers and fathers were telling their children. What a distinguished looking man — slight of build, short, with glasses, the most memorable thing about him was his long, white hair. He was ahead of his time!

In the summer, my wife Erma and I often drive through his hometown, Albion, Michigan, on our way to our cabin in Quebec.

I never drive through there but what I am tempted to look up the Chamber of Commerce and upbraid them for not identifying Albion on their city limits signs as THE HOME OF GEORGE BENNARD, COMPOSER OF AMERICA'S FAVORITE HYMN, "THE OLD RUGGED CROSS." One of these days I'll get up my nerve and make that suggestion.

Speaking of Winona Lake and George Bennard, one cannot go on without mentioning Homer Rodeheaver who, more than anyone else, popularized "The Old Rugged Cross." Traveling around the country with Billy Sunday, Mr. Rodeheaver's rendition of it was par excellence. Of course, his music publishing company was nearby so I seldom came to Winona Lake without seeing and talking with him. Like George Bennard, Mr. Rodeheaver was not tall, but he was more stocky than Mr. Bennard. Both had one thing in common: huge smiles. They seemed eternally happy to me.

I also heard Mr. Rodeheaver sing often in those days. One of my favorites by him was "Then Jesus Came." He wrote the music to those tender Oswald J. Smith lyrics.

22

> One sat alone beside the highway begging,
> His eyes were blind, the light he could not see;
> He clutched his rags and shivered in the shadows,
> Then Jesus came and bade his darkness flee.

> *When Jesus comes the tempter's power is broken;*
> *When Jesus comes the tears are wiped away.*
> *He takes the gloom and fills the life with glory,*
> *For all is changed when Jesus comes to stay.*

Not only did Homer Rodeheaver do great justice to that song with his rich baritone voice, he added much meaning by acting out certain portions as he sang: "One sat alone" . . . "blinded and could not see" . . . "clutched his rags" . . . "tears are wiped away. . . ."

When I heard him, he also did part of the hymn in narration — a dramatic, memorable rendition.

It was a great thrill to meet Mr. Rodeheaver in person. The first time I can recall hearing him was on a record when I was fourteen and living in Ottawa, Canada. Across the street from our Metcalf Street parsonage, I heard this beautiful duet singing "Sunrise." It was coming from the front porch of the Beardsleys. (Mr. Beardsley owned a shoe store in Ottawa.)

I ran over to hear the end of it, and asked if they would play it again. Winding up the mahogany Victrola — something of a show piece at that time — Mr. Beardsley set the needle back at the beginning, and I listened to Homer Rodeheaver and a Mrs. Asher combine their beautiful voices:

> When I shall come to the end of my way,
> When I shall rest at the close of life's day,
> When "Welcome home" I shall hear Jesus say,
> O that will be sunrise for me!

There are so many people who come to mind when I think of those visits to Winona Lake. People such as Virgil and Blanche Brock, whose singing and hymn writing has blessed millions. They were often in attendance during summer meetings at the Billy Sunday pavilion.

It was beautiful Winona Lake which helped inspire their most famous hymn, "Beyond the Sunset." The Brocks were prolific composers whose writing reportedly came most often on inspiration. A phrase from a sermon, a fragment of conversation, a reading from Scripture, some beautiful sight from nature, might set this great husband and wife team in the mood for writing, and they would interrupt whatever they were doing. More than once they reportedly awakened in the middle of the night and inspired by some thought, would write together until morning, Mrs. Brock the music, Mr. Brock the words.

"Beyond the Sunset" was penned in 1936, about the time I first started visiting the Indiana retreat center for WMBI. According to the oft-repeated story, the Brocks were guests of Mr. Rodeheaver, staying at his home on Rainbow Point. After dinner, the Brocks and other guests sat watching a breathtaking sunset across the lake. One of the guests, Horace Burr, a blind man, surprised the group when he said, "I've never seen a more beautiful sunset!"

"How can you say that?" Virgil Brock inquired.

"I see through the eyes of others," he answered. "I even see beyond the sunset."

The combination of the beautiful reflection of the sun across the lake and Mr. Burr's comment triggered Mr. Brock's mind. "Beyond the sunset," he repeated. "Beyond the sunset." The second time he began to hum a tune, improvising other words as he did. Blanche Brock heard him, quietly excused herself and walked into the house where on Mr. Rodeheaver's piano, she fleshed out the melody her husband had begun.

When Mrs. Brock died in 1958, she was buried in Warsaw, Indiana. There in that cemetery on her stone are carved the words and music to one of the world's all-time favorite songs, "Beyond the Sunset."

> Beyond the sunset, O blissful morning,
> When with our Saviour heaven is begun.
> Earth's toiling ended, O glorious dawning,
> Beyond the sunset, when day is done.

C. Austin Miles, composer of "In the Garden," B. D. Ackley, composer of many loved hymns, and Mrs. Charles Cowman, who with her husband edited that famous devotional, *Streams in the Desert* all come to mind when I think of my visits to Winona Lake.

Erma and I first met Mr. Ackley on our honeymoon. Married in 1934 in Ottawa, we made the traditional trip to Niagara Falls, New York, after the wedding. There, one day we visited the famous Churchill Tabernacle from which emanated the popular "Back Home Hour." The Reverend B. D. Ackley was the pianist on the program. An Englishman, who had found the Lord in an American Keswick meeting in New Jersey, he went on to write and play for Homer Rodeheaver, Mr. Ackley's great music will inspire men for many years to come.

Recently, I had opportunity to talk with Mrs. Herbert Dye, Mr. Ackley's daughter who now makes her home at Winona Lake. Reminiscing about the musical work of her father and uncle, Mrs. Dye called to mind many Ackley-written hymns including 'Amazed" and one that was featured often by Dr. Charles Fuller on his "Old Fashioned Revival Hour" — "When I Kneel Down to Pray."

Mrs. Cowman's presence at Winona Lake brings to mind an excerpt from *Streams in the Desert* which I memorized when I was living in Jersey City, outside New York. One day Mother handed me the book with a passage marked. "Maybe you'd like to commit this to memory," she said. "It's a beautiful thought."

I agreed and did memorize it, and can still recite it:

Get up early, go to the mountains and watch God make a morning. The dull gray will give way as God pushes the sun toward the horizon and there will be tints and hues of every shade as the full orbed sun bursts into view. And as the king of the day moves forward majestically flooding the earth and every lowly vale, listen to the music of heaven's choir as it sings of the majesty of God and the glory of the morning. In the hush of the earthly dawn, I hear a voice saying, "I am with you all the day, Rejoice! Rejoice!"

One of my pet peeves is that many of our schools don't encourage more memory work. I think it is a good discipline, and furthermore, it can be a great joy in later years to recall some meaningful poem, a verse of song, Scripture or quote from great literature. I recommend learning some things by heart!

Before I wandered off (I'll be doing that often in this book), and got to talking about "The Old Rugged Cross," George Bennard and my first meeting of him at Winona Lake, I was reminiscing about my childhood music experiences. As I told you, Mother's great love of music was infectious and she, more than anyone else, is responsible for stirring my interest, fanning the coals inside me, and encouraging me to try. Thinking back to those days when she taught me the chords and worked with me at the piano, I realize how important a role parents play in pointing children, unearthing some God-given talent and giving a child confidence in that area. A big kid, awkward, unsure, timid, shy, I needed some field in which I felt comfortable, and music proved to be that field. It is hard for me to imagine — now — that I would have gone any other direction, but in retrospect I see clearly that Mother was the impetus behind my gravitation to music as a life's work.

When I was about eight, I contracted a mysterious throat infection which kept me out of school much of the third and fourth grades. Infected tonsils seemed to be the root of the problem and they were removed, but apparently the poison from them had spread throughout my whole system and the aftereffects lingered for months and months. Today, I suppose penicillin would clear up such a problem in a matter of days. Then, I was put to bed and told to rest.

Mother became my schoolteacher and the kitchen my classroom. While she would cook and bake, I'd sit at the table reading or reciting. She would come over occasionally to give me some help when I got stuck on a word or arithmetic problem. Mother thought one could learn to read as well from the Bible as any other book so I was often given this Book to use. I also read poems (usually of a spiritual nature) and upon occasion, she

Adoration

Mrs. A. J. S.   Mrs. A. J. Shea

1. My Je - sus, Sav - iour, Friend and glor - ious King; Help me to praise Thee and help me to sing Of Thy a - bound - ing grace and love to me, Un - worth - y, poor and sin - ful tho' I be.

2. O praise the Sav - iour, who from hea - ven came! All that's with - in me bless His ho - ly Name! May Christ shine thru me, may my life be pure, My eye be sin - gle and my foot - steps sure.

3. Thy love is won - der - ful, Thy good - ness great; But may we not for - get it till too late. Oh, may none ev - er spurn Thy lov - ing call, But glad - ly yield to Thee, dear Lord, their all.

would ask me to read the verses from a hymnal. Sometimes, moved by a particular hymn, Mother would take me into the living room, where our Bell piano sat, and play and sing the song to me. Then she would ask me to try it. Though I was no child prodigy, I could hack my way through a song at a fairly early age and because of her coaching and compliments, I kept prac-ticing — and improving.

My sisters Pauline and Mary also played the piano. Encouraged by Dad, the whole family was often gathered around the keyboard. The Bell piano was second only to the kitchen table as a family gathering place.

My mother was not surprised by my early interest in music, though. She had taken to it at a young age herself, prompted by God-fearing, music-loving parents. The fact that she composed a hymn herself in her teens is evidence of her seriousness. The number was called "Adoration." I recorded it in an album called *More Songs of the Southland* and you'll see from the accompanying music it is full of meaning and beauty.

I was exposed to music on every hand. In addition to singing and chording at the piano, I also put in a stint on the violin. The fact that my parents put out thirteen dollars for a violin for me from their very limited finances is convincing evidence that music had a high standing on their list of priorities!

Dad liked the violin, and could play it quite well, I discovered. Only his repertoire was limited to square-dance music which he played as a young man. By this time, though, those Saturday night hoedowns were a thing of the past. One of Dad's violin favorites which I can remember him playing was "Turkey in the Straw." Somehow it was out of character for him, however, and after a few bars, he would laugh and hand the instrument back to me.

I wasn't very good on "Turkey in the Straw," but I did learn "Somewhere a Voice Is Calling" and "Absent" which I used to entertain a beautiful young gal named Erma Scharfe. Eventually, she agreed to marry me and she has been putting up with me for nearly thirty-six years now. That may be because I put up the violin! I do have that old violin in my possession again. My brother Alton found it in his attic not long ago and gave it to me.

The first time I played the violin in public came at a month-long camp meeting in Westport, Ontario. I'd gone there with Fred and Kitty Suffield, evangelist friends of my parents who had invited me to go along and help them. As I was about seventeen, I imagine I was invited more out of the kindness of their hearts than for the contribution I might make.

28

What a great team they were! Fred always said that Kitty was sent to him by a Providential snowstorm. He explained by telling how he was awakened by a pounding at his farmhouse door one stormy winter night. When he answered the door, a near-freezing man told him that he was a passenger from a train that had become marooned in the heavy snow. Others on the train were in danger of freezing. Fred dressed hurriedly, lit a lantern and followed the man across snow-covered fields to the stranded passengers. There, he invited them to take shelter at his farm, and many went with him to safety. One of his grateful guests that night was Kitty, who later wrote to thank him for his kindness. A correspondence followed and eventually they fell in love and married.

At a Westport meeting, as I related in *Then Sings My Soul,* I made my first attempt as a vocal soloist. To the accompaniment of Kitty, I sang "He Died of a Broken Heart" — or tried to sing it! I cracked on one of the high notes, but Kitty just kept smiling and played on. I was embarrassed to tears, but when I suggested that I better not try any more solos, she would not hear of it. The next time I sang it in a lower key, and I didn't crack. Still, I never hear those words but what I don't wince. Learning to sing, developing the confidence to hit the high notes and the low ones takes much practice, I learned — painfully. No wonder I remember my first solo.

> *He died of a broken heart — for me,*
> *He died of a broken heart,*
> *O wonderous thought how can it be,*
> *He died of a broken heart.*

Though Fred Suffield has gone home to be with the Lord he preached so effectively about, Kitty is still living — in Los Angeles. I try to see her or give her a call whenever I'm in the area. She wrote many gospel songs that I like, including "Little Is Much."

> **In the harvest fields now ripened**
> **There's a work for all to do,**
> **Hark! The voice of God is calling**
> **"To the harvest," calling you.**

> Little is much when God is in it,
> Labor not for wealth or fame
> There's a crown and you can win it
> When you go in Jesus' name.

> *Does the place we're called to labor*
> *Seem so small and little known?*
> *It is great when God is in it*
> *And He'll not forget His own.*

But her most famous composition (written with her husband) and one that is a particular favorite of mine is "God Is Still on the Throne."

> God is still on the throne
> And He will remember His own,
> Though trials may press us
> And burdens distress us
> He never will leave us alone. . . .

Back in Ottawa after that confidence-building summer with Fred and Kitty, I began to sing more in public. I joined up with three other students who loved to sing and we formed a quartet. One of the guys, our first tenor, was Alonzo Scharfe and it was through his friendship that I met his sister, Erma.

I'll never forget that they put us on the program the day the prestigious Christian and Missionary Alliance Church was dedicated. Before 2,500 people including the mayor, we sang "Come Over Into the Land of Corn and Wine."

> *Come over, come over*
> *To the land of corn and wine,*
> *There's nothing to compare*
> *With the hidden treasures there. . . .*

When we got to the last chorus, we were going so fast we nearly ran right through the land of corn and wine, but by some miracle we finished together. Maybe it was answered prayer. I know Mother and Dad were present that day, and I'm sure Mother began praying when our quartet started speeding. Anyway, we tried and did well enough that our spirit was not broken.

30

When I think back to the kindnesses of people who tolerated my early fumblings I realize how important it is for adults to temper criticism with understanding and patience — otherwise, I would have been washed out of the musical field at an early age.

Churches who find places for young pianists and soloists in their services are to be commended. I know it is a temptation to work with older, more accomplished musicians, but encouraging young people and giving them an opportunity to develop their God-given talents is most important. Not long ago, I heard some young people sing a modern folk-hymn in church to the accompaniment of a guitar. Not only were the lyrics moving, but the guitar was a beautiful addition. New forms of music should not be excluded from church, especially when they are meaningful to young people.

Some of the music I hear today sounds strange to my ears, but I try to keep an open mind to all varieties, realizing that too often we reject the unfamiliar without a fair trial. It's human nature to say we don't like what we don't know, but it's wisdom and a sign of eternal youth to give new things a chance.

On the subjects of young people and gospel music, I might interject right here what to me are the most important qualifications for people involved with music of a spiritual bent. I receive letters regularly from young people asking for career advice.

I'd like to become a singer of gospel hymns as my lifework; how do I proceed?

I like to write religious poetry, and think I'd like to write lyrics for hymns; how do I go about it?

I play the piano and plan to study it in college. Is there a place in the sacred music field for a professional pianist?

Though most of the inquiries I receive are very subjective — matters which will take time and application and prayer to resolve — there are some basic considerations. One of these has to do with degree of involvement. To become a minister of the gospel, one needs to attend a seminary and prepare himself for his calling.

31

To become a Christian worker, one needs to study the Bible and have some understanding of Scripture before he can talk to someone else about his faith, but his degree of training will seldom be as intensive as an ordained minister's. Much the same is true of the gospel music field. People on the Billy Graham musical team such as Cliff Barrows, Tedd Smith and John Innes have prepared themselves professionally for their ministries. People who direct local church choirs or sing in them, organists or pianists may or may not have college degrees in music, but they are students of the hymns and continue to grow in their abilities by practicing. The point I'm trying to make is, that there are many ways of serving God through music, but whether professional or part-time, all callings make certain demands. There are at least four qualifications that I think essential:

First, to sing the words of the hymns with conviction, one needs to believe that they are true. Whole-heartedness is essential. Without belief, the power of the lyrics fades. It's not hard to tell from listening to someone sing whether or not he or she is attuned with the words of a song.

Second, a mechanical one: You must have the ability to carry a tune if you're going to be an effective music witness. If you have no sense of melody, your area of service no doubt lies in another direction, but most of us have been given about the same physical equipment. The difference is in the development of it, which brings me to:

Third, you must be willing to work, listen, be taught, practice and apply yourself if you are going to improve. This is true in any discipline and music is no exception. I figure I have been "going to school" for better than forty years, and every day I learn something new from the people with whom I come in contact. Don Hustad, who is now a professor at the Southern Baptist Seminary in Louisville, is a good example. Though he is one of the most knowledgeable people in the field of sacred music that I know, he never has stopped learning.

A person who wants to be a part of this field must love music very much.

Fourth (and maybe most important), gospel music needs people who want to give themselves to a cause, namely the work of Jesus

Christ. There is no room for peacocks who make attention-getting shrieks or grand displays of their beautiful feathers. Working in the religious music field is not *show business,* but *God business,* and unless you can subordinate your own ego, it's probably best you use your talent in another way. That saying which I've seen on so many pulpits—one that faces the singer or speaker—is apropos: WE WOULD SEE JESUS.

I remember the first time I played the organ in public. It was at the Fifth Avenue Church in Ottawa. Though it was a small reed organ, it really captivated me. It had more tonal range than any reed organ I'd ever played. I particularly liked the celeste stop which cancelled the lefthand bass. One of my chums, Asa MacIntosh, managed to get permission for me to play it occasionally and he would listen appreciatively while I practiced.

It was a beautiful Estey reed organ that produced some heavenly *vox humana* sounds. When I played "Safe in the Arms of Jesus," Asa called up from where he was sitting, "Boy, Bev, that is really terrific. You sound great."

Lest anyone think Asa and I spent all our time in church, however, let me dispel that notion by telling you how we occasionally passed time after supper.

Hiding in the bushes along Bank Street, we would plant an empty wallet on the sidewalk and attach fishing tackle to it. Then we'd wait in the bushes until somebody would come along and spot the billfold. When he or she would bend down to pick it up, we'd give the line a jerk and reel it in. That was our idea of devilment.

How shaken I was when Asa became ill at age fifteen, suffering from some heart malfunction. Within a few weeks he wasted away from what appeared to be fine health to death.

When word came that he had died, his mother asked me if I would play the organ at his funeral. "Asa told me how beautiful you play 'Safe in the Arms of Jesus.' Would you do that hymn for us?"

I agreed. At age fifteen, I drew one of the toughest assignments I've ever had, but I'm sure that hymn was a comfort to Asa's family as it has been to so many at times of bereavement. The words offer wonderful reassurance:

> *Safe in the arms of Jesus,*
> *Safe on His gentle breast*
> *There by His love o'ershadowed,*
> *Sweetly my soul shall rest.*

I have never forgotten that Ottawa organ. "Some day I'm going to own one of my own," I told Erma when we were still dating. Well, many, many years later while I was reading the *Chicago Tribune* one morning I saw an ad for reed organs. I followed it up, and went to the home of an old man on Chicago's North Side. There in his basement were dozens of old organs including an Estey just like the one I played in Asa's church. It was the exact same model — made in about 1915 I'd guess — about four feet high and five feet wide.

Pressing the keys and hitting a chord, I could tell it was in excellent condition. Then, I noticed that celeste stop which created that haunting sound of muted strings. I anxiously pulled the stop and began to play "Safe in the Arms of Jesus." There it was, that magnificent tone. I completely forgot myself and played and sang a whole verse of that hymn.

Then, I heard the man shuffle his feet before self-consciously asking, "You like it?"

"Yes, I do."

"Well, she's yours for sixty-five dollars." I would have paid him much more.

Today, it occupies a corner of our basement. I have stripped all the panels from it, have removed the varnish and am refinishing it. Erma says I can bring it upstairs into our recreation room when I complete the job — which will be some time around 1985 at my present pace.

Meanwhile, I content myself with a few chords every time I go to the basement on some mundane chore quite incongruous with the ethereal sounds which come from my prized Estey.

In 1967, I recorded "Safe in the Arms of Jesus" for RCA. I included it in an album called *Be Still My Soul*.

After the album was finished but before it was released, I flew to New York to attend a testimonial luncheon arranged by The National Association of Recording Arts and Sciences to honor Steve Sholes, an RCA vice-president who was my first A & R (Artist and Repertoire) man. He worked with such superstars as Eddy Arnold, Chet Atkins, and Elvis Presley. The next day following the luncheon, I went to Steve's office to hear my soon-to-be-released album. After Steve and I had heard "Safe in the Arms of Jesus," he told me how much the words meant to him.

It was not an offhand comment. He had come forward to make a public confession during our Pittsburgh Crusade. His decision, his comment about "Safe in the Arms of Jesus" and all his kindnesses to me returned to mind a few weeks later when I received word in Australia that Steve Sholes, one of the most beloved men in the recording industry, had died of a heart attack in Nashville.

As most know, "Safe in the Arms of Jesus," is a William H. Doane-Fanny Crosby hymn. It was written in 1869 in New York City. Reportedly, Mr. Doane brought the music to Mrs. Crosby and asked her to write words for it.

"Let me hear it," she said. The blind woman sat attentively listening while he played his composition on a small organ. When he had finished Mrs. Crosby told him:

"That says we are safe in the arms of Jesus. Let me see what I can do with it." Half an hour later, she was back with the lyrics as we know them more than a hundred years hence.

Incidentally, in that same year, Mr. Doane gave Mrs. Crosby another tune which was to gain great favor in gospel hymn circles. To that music she set the words to "Jesus, Keep Me Near the Cross."

> In the cross, in the cross
> Be my glory ever,
> Till my raptured soul shall find
> Rest beyond the river.

Speaking of Steve Sholes' decision at Pittsburgh brings to mind my own commitment to Christ. All my brothers and sisters had turned their lives over to the Lord except me. Though I was a believer, I had not made a public statement to that effect—and when I still hadn't at age eighteen, I suppose my family became a little concerned. I know why I hadn't gone forward: I was just too shy.

Then Kitty and Fred Suffield came to Dad's church in Ottawa for revival services. Dad was preaching when Fred found the Lord. He went into evangelistic work in part because of Dad's encouragement so they were especially close friends. Each night I attended the service and each night at the altar call I would sing the songs of invitation fervently and passionately, but did not budge from my spot in the very last pew.

"Oh, Why Not Tonight," "I Am Praying for You," "Let the Saviour In," "Only Trust Him," "Pass Me Not," "Almost Persuaded"—I sang them all without surrendering. Finally, on the last night of special services, I went forward to the music that has served as background for millions of similar decisions.

> Just as I am, without one plea,
>   But that Thy blood was shed for me,
> And that Thou bidd'st me come to Thee,
>   O Lamb of God, I come! I come!
>
> Just as I am, and waiting not
>   To rid my soul of one dark blot,
> To Thee whose blood can cleanse each spot,
>   O Lamb of God, I come! I come!
>
> Just as I am, though tossed about
>   With many a conflict, many a doubt,
> Fightings and fears within, without,
>   O Lamb of God, I come! I come!
>
> Just as I am, poor, wretched, blind;
>   Sight, riches, healing of the mind,
> Yea, all I need, in Thee I find,
>   O Lamb of God, I come! I come!

> Just as I am, Thou wilt receive,
>   Wilt welcome, pardon, cleanse, relieve;
> Because Thy promise I believe,
>   O Lamb of God, I come! I come!

"Just As I Am" is probably the most famous invitational hymn of them all. We use it often in our Crusades because it says it all.

It has an interesting story behind its writing.

In 1836, lyricist Charlotte Elliott, a Londoner and a person of no little musical education, suffered a breakdown and became bedridden at age thirty-three. When a minister came to visit her he inquired if she were a Christian. The woman said in effect that that was a matter between her and God. But a few weeks later, she invited him back and in a more contrite spirit asked:

"How does one come to Christ?"

"Why, just come to Him as you are," the minister answered. And that is what she did. Fourteen years later, looking back on that turning point in her life, she wrote the words which were set to music by William Bradbury.

Someone asked me one day why only the choir sings the invitation hymn at Crusades. I had an answer.

One day I told Billy Graham about my conversion experience, noting that "I think I was actually finding release from the conviction I was under by singing good and loud. Instead of going forward, I *sang*."

"That's very interesting, Bev," he said.

That night when the organist began playing the invitational hymn, I was pleasantly surprised to hear Billy say, "Now while the *choir* is singing 'Just As I Am' . . . ."

Songs That Led to a Life's Work

"What do you think you'd like to do with your life, Son?" Dad asked me one day toward the end of my high-school years.

I told him I wasn't sure, but that I hoped to find the answer at Houghton College. I already had made plans to enroll there in a general course of study, and though I hoped to sing in the glee club as an extra curricular activity, the thought of pursuing a career in music didn't enter my head. First of all, I had very little confidence in my voice or my ability to use it. Second, no one I knew was making a living singing or playing gospel hymns. No, I'd have to find some utilitarian job. I did hope to serve the Lord in some way, but in what way I wasn't sure. One thing of which I was certain: I would never be a minister.

I was so shy, so tongue-tied and such a mumbler when I stood to speak that no one ever suggested I might some day follow in Dad's footsteps, and I certainly never entertained the idea.

There followed a memorable year at Houghton College—a year only, because it was 1928–29 and there just wasn't enough money to continue. But it was another link in my training. Professor Herman Baker gave me some vocal help that has proved valuable. He always advised pupils that they should study their music until it became a part of their heart and soul.

It was another way of saying, "Anything worth doing is worth doing right." My Scriptural injunction for striving for perfection comes from 2 Timothy 2:15: *Study to shew thyself approved unto God, a workman that needeth not be ashamed. . . .*

One number I learned to love that year was "Remember Now Thy Creator" and though it was beyond my capabilities then I eventually learned it and have used it upon occasion. I love its thought, drawn from Ecclesiastes 11:9.

> Rejoice, O young man, in thy youth; and let thy heart cheer thee in the days of thy youth, and walk in the ways of thine heart, and in the sight of thine eyes; but know thou that for all these things God will bring thee into judgment.

Family financial problems limited my college to one year, 1928–29. I decided to work a while and then return, but as they say, "One thing led to another," and it never happened.

Dad had accepted a call to a Jersey City church outside New York City so I went to join my family there. I soon had a job working in the medical department of Mutual of New York (MONY), the life insurance company. I went to work for them just two months before the stock market crash, and stayed there almost nine years.

Meanwhile, I kept busy with my singing and playing. Mother and I alternated Sundays at church, playing an old motorized reed organ. I spent hours each week preparing music to be in the service, the designated hymns, the invitation, the offertory. One of my favorite offertory numbers was:

> **Have Thine own way, Lord, have Thine own way!**
> **Thou art the Potter; I am the clay,**
> **Mould me and make me after Thy will,**
> **While I am waiting, yielded and still.**

The music for this great hymn was written in 1907 by George C. Stebbins, a wonderful Christian composer whom I got to meet a few years later.

That was in 1943. I helped Jack Wyrtzen with his evangelistic work that summer and one day he invited me to go with him to visit Mr. Stebbins, who at age ninety-five was retired and living with a relative in the Catskills. What a pleasure to meet him. Though hard-of-hearing, he was very alert and pleased to have visitors. A tall man with whiskers, he exuded great dignity and warmth. Jack introduced us and suggested I sing "There is a Green Hill Far Away," one of Mr. Stebbins's many musical contributions. (The words were written by Cecil F. Alexander) and while others have put this poem to music, Stebbins's version is the most requested.

"Get close to his ear, Bev," Jack coached and I did as I sang:

> There is a green hill far away
> Without a city wall,
> Where my dear Lord was crucified
> Who died to save us all.
>
> O dearly, dearly, has He loved
> And we must love Him, too,
> And trust in His redeeming blood
> And try His work to do.

When I had finished, Mr. Stebbins smiled and nodded his head.

"Wonderful. A fine job. Your voice reminds me of my friend Carlton Booth."

I thanked him for the compliment. Being compared to a fine singer like Carlton was high praise indeed. However, Jack had all he could do to keep from laughing out loud, and seeing him cover his face almost broke me up. The joke was that Carlton Booth is a high tenor and I'm a bass baritone or so they tell me. Mr. Stebbins's deafness aside, he meant well, and I accepted his comment as the compliment it was intended.

I will never forget the moving prayer he gave before Jack and I left. Taking our hands, he prayed:

"Dear Lord, we thank Thee for this visit from Thy servants. Thank You for gospel music, the inspiration it gives. And thank You for sending these people — Mr. Wyrtzen and Mr. Shea who love to tell others about You through sermons and song. Thank You for the music You placed on my heart and for letting me serve You through music. Bless these men, guide them and strengthen them as they carry on the work that others before them have begun. We give You the glory. In Jesus's Name, Amen."

That day Mr. Stebbins gave me an autographed copy of his book, *Reminiscences and Gospel Hymn Stories* which I cherish very much to this day. The pen shook so hard as he signed the book that he needed to steady it with his other hand, but I had to admire his marvelous spirit. Incidentally, the book, which was published in 1924, is a treasury of fascinating gospel hymn stories, dating from 1869 when Mr. Stebbins's talent and Christian dedication were first recognized by many well-known religious figures at that time. He wrote the melody for hundreds of hymns, some of which are still favorites. To Mr. Stebbins's credit are such tunes as "Saviour, Breathe An Evening Blessing" (or "Evening Prayer"), "Ye Must Be Born Again" (with W. T. Sleeper) and that wonderful, old invitational "Jesus, I Come," also written with Mr. Sleeper:

> **Out of my bondage, sorrow and night,**
> **Jesus, I come, Jesus, I come,**
> **Into Thy freedom, gladness and light**
> **Jesus, I come to Thee.**
> **Out of my sickness into Thy health,**
> **Out of my want and into Thy wealth**
> **Out of my sin and into Thyself**
> **Jesus I come to Thee.**

Mr. Stebbins also wrote the music for "True Hearted, Whole Hearted," "Take Time to Be Holy" and several of Aunt Fanny Crosby's poems such as "Jesus Is Tenderly Calling" and "Saved by Grace"—two hymns I haven't heard lately. They deserve remembering. Many a lost soul has made his way on an altar of prayer while singing:

> Jesus is tenderly calling thee home,
> Calling today, calling today;
> Why from the sunshine of love wilt thou roam,
> Farther and farther away?
>
> *Calling today, calling today*
> *Jesus is calling, Is tenderly calling today.*

And how many times have you sung these words?

> Some day the silver chord will break
> And I no more as now shall sing;
> But O, the joy when I shall wake
> Within the palace of the King!
>
> *And I shall see Him face to face,*
> *And tell the story — Saved by grace;*
> *And I shall see Him face to face*
> *And tell the story — Saved by grace.*

How exciting to read through Mr. Stebbins's memoirs as he recalls his travels and ministry with Dwight L. Moody, Major D. W. Whittle, Philip P. Bliss, Ira D. Sankey, William H. Doane, James McGranahan, William Kirkpatrick, Rev. George F. Pentecost, George Root, H. R. Palmer, and many other evangelical leaders of the day.

The book is full of insight into the personalities and characters of many Christians whose contributions to God's work are well known, but whose lives are not. For example, I read with interest a passage which told about Mr. Stebbins's last meeting with Philip P. Bliss, one of the giants of gospel hymn writing ("Almost Persuaded," "Wonderful Words of Life," "Hallelujah," "What a Saviour," "Let the Lower Lights Be Burning," "The Light of the World is Jesus"). Wrote Mr. Stebbins:

> I was appointed [by D. L. Moody] to assist George C. Needham
> in his work in Oshkosh, Wisconsin, and later, with Charles Inglis
> of England, I was sent to one of the smaller churches of South
> Chicago. On entering the railway station on my way to this second

appointment, I found Mr. and Mrs. Bliss waiting for the train I was to take.

While bidding goodbye to Mrs. Stebbins and our son, then a small boy, Mr. and Mrs. Bliss were reminded of their two boys in the home of friends in Rome, Pennsylvania, and tears came to their eyes.

After leaving Chicago, Mr. Bliss fell asleep, with his head resting on his wife's shoulder. He was still sleeping when my destination was reached. As I rose to pass out, I said to Mrs. Bliss, "Don't disturb him." She replied: "Oh, yes! He would be disappointed if he did not say goodbye." As he wakened and realized I was leaving, he followed me onto the platform with kindest wishes and parting words.

This proved to be the last time I saw him, for he and Mrs. Bliss at the conclusion of the meetings at Peoria, went to their children to spend the holidays, and on their way back to Chicago, a few days later, they met their tragic death at Ashtabula, Ohio.

Reminiscences and Gospel Hymn Stories

The death of Mr. and Mrs. Bliss on December 29, 1876 was indeed tragic. Mr. Bliss was just thirty-eight and at the time was producing some of his best hymns. A writer of words and music, and a soloist and song leader as well (he often conducted services with Major Whittle), Mr. Bliss is described as handsome, tall and with a strong, moving bass baritone voice. Yet, friends seemed to be more impressed with his gentleness than anything else. They mourned in great numbers when he and his wife lost their lives in a fiery train wreck. Reportedly, Mr. Bliss survived the crash and climbed through a broken window to safety, but then returned to the coach trying to rescue his wife. Neither got out. In Mr. Bliss' effects was found a copy of an unpublished hymn he had recently completed:

> **I will sing of my Redeemer**
> **And His wondrous love to me;**
> **On the cruel cross He suffered,**
> **From the curse to set me free.**

43

I will tell the wondrous story,
　How my lost estate to save,
In His boundless love and mercy,
　He the ransom freely gave.

I will praise my dear Redeemer,
　His triumphant power I'll tell,
How the victory He giveth
　Over sin, and death, and hell.

I will sing of my Redeemer
　And His heavenly love for me;
He from death to life hath brought me,
　Son of God, with Him to be.

Sing, oh, sing of my Redeemer,
　With His blood He purchased me,
On the cross He sealed my pardon,
　Paid the debt, and made me free.

I was telling you about those early days in New York City where I was working for an insurance company and living with Mother and Dad in Jersey City, playing the organ at the Wesleyan Church. It was that organ which was used to introduce the first hymn I ever wrote. Once again Mother — my musical guardian — had a part.

A lover of beauty be it a flower, a bird, a poem, an ennobling quotation — whatever — Mother was a collector. What she collected most, though, was friends. A person who gave herself without qualification to others, she won so many to her with her warmth, her wit, and her charm.

With friends and family she loved to share poetry and she always had some verse in hand copied from a book or clipped from a magazine. As I've told before, it was her practice of leaving such writing on the piano music rack which led to my writing "I'd Rather Have Jesus" when I was twenty. The same Sunday morning I read those wonderful words for the first time I wrote music for them and used the song that same day in my father's church service. Of course, Mrs. Rhea F. Miller is the catalyst. Without her inspiring lyrics, there would have been no song.

A copy of Bev Shea's most famous composition in his hand. (Copyright assigned to Chancel Music, Inc.)

That's true with a number of our church classics. Without the faith and talented pen of such poets as Longfellow, Phillips Brooks, William Cullen Bryant, Oliver Wendell Holmes, Martin Luther, Henry Van Dyke, Charles Wesley, Isaac Watts, Thomas Moore, Rudyard Kipling, John Milton, Alfred Tennyson, William Wordsworth and other famous writers, we would have been denied the joy of many a great hymn.

Over the years, I've not sung any song more than "I'd Rather Have Jesus," but I never tire of Mrs. Miller's heartfelt words.

All those years in New York, I studied voice and gained experience by singing in church choirs and on radio. Like so many things in life, all of these opportunities were jig-saw puzzle pieces that eventually fit into a pattern—though that pattern was very vague then.

One of the first men I studied under lived in the West Seventies. I can't remember his name which is just as well. Though well qualified, his goals and mine were far different, and we soon parted company.

For a few weeks, I rode the subway uptown to take lessons but in addition to not being *simpatico* to gospel music, this man nearly broke me—financially. For twenty minutes of instruction (and he practically set an alarm clock to make sure he didn't give me any extra time) he charged ten dollars. That was about a third of my salary then. My seriousness about music is reflected in the fact that I went to him at all.

I had better luck with his successors—the likes of Emerson Williams and Price Boone. I'll never forget my audition with Emerson Williams, who sang bass on NBC with the famous Revelers Quartet. He was some kind of singer. What a voice! He asked me to do something I liked and I pulled the music to "The Love of God" out of my case. After I had sung it, he had tears in his eyes and some kind words for me. He agreed to take me on as a student, and I was pleased, though I had a feeling my selection of music had as much to do with his decision as my voice.

Speaking of Frederick M. Lehman's great hymn "The Love of God" reminds me of something I learned about it not long ago. Rumor had it that the third verse lyrics were found on the walls of an institution about the time this popular hymn was written in 1917. Though this could be true, the roots of it go back to the eleventh century, at least, and maybe further. According to my information, a modern-day translation of the verse was made by Rabbi Joseph Marcus from the Aramaic. A close approximation of the verse is used one day each year in the Jewish observance of *Shavuot* (Festival of Weeks) which begins seven weeks after Passover.

But without Mrs. Lehman there would be no song. Like Mother's habit of placing poems and notes on the piano for me, Frederick Lehman's wife put such findings in her husband's lunch pail. Mr. Lehman was a minister, but because most of his churches were small and could pay him little, he worked at various jobs to support his family. One of these jobs was in a cheese factory, and it was there that Mr. Lehman got his inspiration for "The Love of God." His wife had come into possession of a poem which began, "Could we with ink the ocean fill. . . ." She put a copy of it in Frederick's lunch pail. He was so moved by the words that he came home that night and worked on a tune to go with them. Later, he wrote two other verses and thus was born another great gospel hymn.

Whatever the third verse's origin it is good to know that Christians and Jews share in the sentiments expressed in these great words of praise to God:

1st verse
The love of God is greater far
Than tongue or pen can ever tell;
It goes beyond the highest star,
And reaches to the lowest hell;
The guilty pair, bowed down with care,
God gave His Son to win;
His erring child, He reconciled,
And pardoned from his sin.

Chorus
Oh, Love of God, how rich and pure!
How measureless and strong!
It shall forevermore endure—
The saints' and angels' song.

3rd verse
Could we with ink the ocean fill,
And were the skies of parchment made;
Were every stalk on earth a quill,
And every man a scribe by trade;
To write the love of God above
Would drain the ocean dry;
Nor could the scroll contain the whole,
Tho' stretched from sky to sky.

After my time with Emerson Williams, I studied with Price Boone who sang tenor in the Calvary Baptist Church choir. An operatic talent, Price once seemed destined for a starring role at the Met, but after his Number One admirer and sponsor Herbert Witherspoon, Met general manager, died, interest in Price waned. He switched to teaching and I was one of his lucky pupils.

I sang in a quartet with Price on Erling C. Olsen's program, "Meditations in the Psalms," over WHN and WMCA. Others in that group were Hassie Mayfield, soprano, and William Miller, top tenor. Our theme song which we used to open and close the program was the eternally beautiful "When Morning Gilds the Skies."

When morning gilds the skies
My heart awaking cries,
May Jesus Christ be praised!
Alike at work and prayer,
To Jesus I repair;
May Jesus Christ be praised!

In those days, Erma often provided skillful accompaniment for me. She studied piano at Toronto Conservatory and her musical ability was one of those additional blessings I got when she agreed to become my wife. I thank God for my girl, Erma, every day.

Another program I sang on at this time was J. Thurston Noé's "Sundown," which was aired each Friday evening. For a couple of years, I did two songs each week on his organ program. Mr. Noé was organist and director of the Calvary Baptist Church choir, a talented musician and composer. The theme of "Sun-

48

down" was Mr. Noé's own beloved "Thou Light of Light."
Such a glorious benediction!

> *The sun goes down, the evening shadows lengthen,*
> *The western hills are rimmed with golden light,*
> *The day is o'er, the twilight glow is fading,*
> *A silent tide flows out into the night.*
> *Though still and deep, the darkness cannot hide Thee*
> *Thou Light of light, shine through the night to me.*

And I remember practicing with Mr. Noé and the Calvary
choir at the church across from Carnegie Hall in preparation
for special services, such as at Christmas or Easter. No one threw
himself into rehearsals any more enthusiastically or more completely than he did. He was greatly praised for his conducting of
Handel's *Messiah* and Dubois' *The Seven Last Words of Christ,*
whenever he presented them. I remember in particular the time
we did *The Seven Last Words* on network radio. What a produc-
tion. In addition to some of the finest voices in New York, Mr.
Noé had brought in several musicians from the Philharmonic to
add to the grandeur. For a little more drama that night, he had
arranged to have the lights turned out during the famous storm
passage. Price Boone sang the tenor aria just before the storm.

Then, the cymbals crashed and the organ thundered. It was the
most effective simulation of a storm I have ever heard. Mr. Noé
directed the choir from the organ, his music lit by a small blue
light. It was the only light in the church, and though dim, I could
make out the expression on his face. How he was enjoying "his
storm!"

Finally, *The Seven Last Words of Christ* reached that final
crescendo:

> **Christ, we do all adore Thee**
> **And we do praise Thee forever.**

When it was over, I caught the triumphant look on Mr. Noé's
face, a look I'll never forget. And there were tears in his eyes —
he was so moved.

At rehearsal for that concert, I remember him telling me one day, "The basses need to come on a little stronger, with more confidence at this point. You lead them, Beverly. When I give you the signal, come in *fortissimo*."

I nodded that I would.

As we sang, Mr. Noé moved across the highly polished floor from one side of the area to the other, coaching the different sections. Just before the part he had mentioned to me, he was on the opposite side leading the sopranos. Suddenly, he turned and dashed in our direction, sliding the last ten feet like an ice skater. As he came to a skidding halt in front of me, he jabbed his index finger in my face and commanded *"Now!"* I was so amused that I broke up as did everyone else in the choir—including Mr. Noé.

The last time I saw him was in Birmingham, Michigan, in 1967. I had a singing date at Detroit's Cobo Hall and I drove out from there to visit him. He and his wife had moved to Michigan to be near his son, Dick, who with some other engineers helped design the famous retractable hardtop for Ford. When I walked into his living room, one of the first things I saw was his Steinway grand piano. I recalled how I used to go out to the Noés' home in South Orange, New Jersey, with others and practice while he accompanied us. Such fantastic music he got out of that instrument, the same one he used to compose on.

We had a great time reminiscing that day. Though showing age, his spirit was still young. Once, he excused himself and went into another room to get some music to play for me. His wife, Mabel, whispered, "He's enjoying himself so much. He hasn't played the piano in over a year."

I couldn't imagine what would keep that lover of music away from his piano, but I learned when I got home where a letter from Mrs. Noé was waiting.

I did not know if I could stand to tell you when you were here, but we lost Dick a year ago. A sudden heart attack. It seemed so unnecessary for one so young . . . When there is only one there is such an awful void left.

50

Their son Dick was just forty-two when he died—on his father's birthday. I was even more pleased that I had been able to visit the Noés after receiving that letter.

A few months later news came from Mrs. Noé that "her Thurston" had died. I was on my way to Australia at the time, and though I talked with her by phone, I was not able to attend the funeral which I regretted.

When I got back home again, Mrs. Noé had a surprise for me. She wrote:

> One day I said, quite casually, not dreaming that he would pass first, "Thurston, what would you want me to do about the piano?" As you know he was always a little slow and deliberate in speaking, but he answered spontaneously and with that spark of pleasant temperament, "My one and only choice would be Bev Shea, but I don't know that he would want it."

Want it! I wrote back immediately to tell Mrs. Noé how honored I would be to have the piano, not only because I've always wanted a grand piano, but because it belonged to a dear friend who used it to compose many outstanding hymns of praise. Today, it occupies a prominent place in our home, and I use it often. I never sit down to play it but what I remember Thurston and the history that the piano represents.

While doing research for this book, I called Mrs. Noé and asked her to send me a picture of Thurston. When she kindly replied, she not only sent along his picture, but a quotation from John Ruskin's *Ethics of the Dust*. It was a favorite of Thurston's and reflects his own personal philosophy, I think. The paper reads:

"Rest"

There is no music in a "rest," but there is the making of music in it.

In our whole life melody, the music is broken off here and there by "rests" and we foolishly think we have come to the end of the tune. God sends a time of forced leisure, sickness, disappointed plans, frustrated efforts that makes a sudden pause in the choral hymn of our lives, and we lament that our voice must be silent and our part missing in the music which ever goes up to the ear of the Creator.

How does the musician read the rest?

See him bèat the time with unvarying count and catch up the next note true and steady as if no breaking place had come in between.

Not without design does God write the music of our lives. But be it ours to learn the time and not be dismayed at the "rests." They are not to be slurred over, not to be omitted, nor to destroy the melody, nor to change the keynote.

If we look up, God, Himself will beat the time for us. With the eye on Him, we shall strike the next note full and clear.

At the bottom of it was an editorial comment by Thurston. He felt that the line which reads "God sends a time of forced leisure, etc. . . ." should read, "There *seems* to be a time of forced leisure, . . ." Thurston's explanation: "We cannot believe a good God would send distress on His child when even a human father would refrain from doing so."

Interesting—how one friendship, one contact, one opportunity leads to another. Mr. Noé introduced me to Price Boone. With Price I sang on Erling C. Olsen's program. Among the guest speakers on that radio hour was Dr. Will Houghton, who after serving as minister at Calvary Baptist went to Chicago to serve as president of Moody Bible Institute. Dr. Houghton is an important link in my life because he was responsible for my entering full-time religious work.

At Pinebrook Bible Conference in the Poconos the summer of 1938, Dr. Houghton asked me if I had ever considered Christian radio as a vocation. I told him quite honestly that I hadn't.

"There's an opening on the staff of WMBI [the Moody Bible Institute Station in Chicago] that I think you could fill," he told me. Before the summer was over I had been hired and was on my way to Chicago.

My wife of four years, Erma—the Ottawa girl I'd courted with my violin—joined me a month later and we thus began a joint adventure that is now into its fourth decade. For the wonderful experiences that have followed that decision I can only respond:

Praise God from Whom all blessings flow,
Praise Him, all creatures here below,
Praise Him above, ye heavenly host,
Praise Father, Son and Holy Ghost.

3

A Full-Time
Ministry of Song

The Christ of Every Road

There's a long road and a weary road
As it winds and twists along,
There are sad men once were glad men,
But silent is their song,
Life is dead, they say
For He went away,
One in whom our hopes were borne,
He was by our side, then crucified,
Now we walk this road forlorn.

Those words were written by Dr. Houghton (the music by Wendell Loveless, former director of WMBI) who conducted a radio program each Sunday called "Let's Go Back to the Bible." Shortly after going to Chicago, I began singing regularly on that program. What a privilege it was to work with Dr. Houghton, a dedicated servant of Christ! In addition to doing "Let's Go Back to the Bible," I sang daily at 8:15 A.M. over WMBI on a program called "Hymns From the Chapel," as I mentioned before.

Occasionally some people stopped by the radio studios to say hello. One of them was a ministerial student at nearby Wheaton College. His name was Billy Graham.

It was only a short time later that I heard him speak—at a Chicago Youth for Christ Rally. That was an exciting night, really the launching of Youth for Christ by Torrey Johnson. A crowd of 2,900 showed up at Orchestra Hall on Michigan Avenue. I remember singing two spirituals that night, "Yes, He Did" and "The Old Time Religion." That young and ecumenical audience particularly liked some adlibbing:

> Give me that old time religion,
> Give me that old time religion,
> It's good enough for me—
> It makes the Baptists love the Methodists,
> Makes the Methodists love the Baptists,
> Makes the Presbyterians love—everybody.

Billy's sermon was on his favorite subject: becoming a Christian. And he convinced a goodly number that it was a good time to do just that.

Meanwhile, I continued studying music (under Gino Monaco) and I was singing at various functions throughout the Midwest. In 1944 through my friendship with Bob Walker (now editor-publisher of *Christian Life*) who was on the board of Club Aluminum headed by Herbert J. Taylor, I was hired to do a daily, fifteen-minute show over WCFL. It was called "Club Time" and when I signed the contract for thirteen weeks it ended my association with WMBI. The station's policy prohibited employees from working commercially, so I had to resign. The move was a gamble, but Erma and I entered it prayerfully and it proved to be the right decision—again.

Eventually, the program went nationwide in September, 1945. It was aired weekly for seven years.

A feature of the show was doing the favorite hymn of a well-known person. I remember singing "In the Garden," Kate Smith's favorite, and "Softly and Tenderly" which was the favorite of my singing idol, John Charles Thomas. It's always been one of my top choices, too. Written by Will Thompson (known as the bard of Ohio) the noted composer once visited Dwight L. Moody

55

near the end of the evangelist's life. Reaching up from his bed, Moody is said to have told Mr. Thompson, "Will, I would rather have written 'Softly and Tenderly' than anything I have been able to do in my whole life." Moody's appreciation of the hymn was prophetic. The relatively new work came to be one of the most popular invitational songs of all time.

> Softly and tenderly Jesus is calling,
> Calling for you and for me,
> See on the portals He's waiting and watching,
> Watching for you and for me.
>
> *Come home, come home,*
> *Ye who are weary, come home;*
> *Earnestly, tenderly, Jesus is calling,*
> *Calling, O sinner, come home!*

I started "Club Time" in 1944 about the same time I agreed to sing on a Sunday evening program called "Songs in the Night" over WCFL. Torrey Johnson had originated the program, but had to give it up because of pressing Youth for Christ commitments. His young prodigy, Billy Graham, who by now was pastor of the Village Church, Western Springs, Illinois, had agreed to succeed him.

Billy came to me and asked if I would sing on the program. Though overcommitted myself, I couldn't say no, especially when I learned that he had volunteered to go without salary in order to get his struggling church to sponsor the program. It was a decision I've never regretted. The name of the program came from that verse in Job 35:10: Forsaken, Job cried out, *Where is God my maker, who giveth songs in the night?*

Each Sunday night a group known as the King's Carolers and I would open the program from Western Springs by singing Wendell P. Loveless's "Songs in the Night."

> *Songs in the night,*
> *The Lord giveth songs in the night,*
> *Sorrows may come, darkness or light*
> *But He giveth songs in the night.*

This is not to be confused with another song which bears the same title. It was written by J. Thurston Noé and Dr. Houghton.

> *What though the hours be long and dreary,*
> *What though the road be hard and weary,*
> *Songs in the night, I'll not fear sorrow,*
> *Songs in the night, and then tomorrow,*
> *The world holds but darkness and Christ is the light,*
> *He giveth songs, songs in the night.*

Those were exciting days but only a shadow of things to come. For Billy Graham there was Youth for Christ work which followed his pastorate at Western Springs. This new endeavor took him all over the country and—in 1946—on a six-month campaign in the British Isles. His song leader for those meetings was a young handsome package of energy named Cliff Barrows.

Upon their return, I received an invitation from Billy to join him, Cliff and an old classmate of Billy's—Grady Wilson—in Charlotte, North Carolina, in November, 1947, for a three-week city-wide rally. I agreed and the foundation for the Crusade work was laid that November in the First Baptist Church on Tryon Street. The crowds were such that we had to move to the armory the final week. The first number I did there—the unofficial launching of the Crusades—was one of Billy's favorites, "I Will Sing the Wondrous Story."

> *I will sing the wondrous story*
> *Of the Christ who died for me*
> *Sing it with the saints in glory*
> *Gathered by the crystal sea.*

Meanwhile, I continued my work in Chicago, concentrating on "Club Time." I joined Billy, Cliff, and Grady for about three campaigns a year in those early days, but it was not until September of 1949 that Billy's ministry took wings. The springboard proved to be the Los Angeles Crusade.

There in a huge tent at Washington Boulevard and Hill Street six thousand people came nightly. The three-week campaign

57

stretched to eight and I sang each night which took some doing. I had to return to Chicago after Monday's service, fly all night, do my "Club Time" stint live on Tuesday morning, then get on a plane and fly all day to get back in time for Tuesday night's service. It was an exhausting schedule, but well worth it.

Some of the people who came forward at the Los Angeles Crusade were famous, and these men and women created news which spread and attracted others. One of those people was a famous personality and songwriter who, after he found Christ, wrote these well-known lyrics:

> It is no secret what God can do,
> What He did for others, He'll do for you.

The author, as most know, is Stuart Hamblen.

Stuart figured in my joining RCA a short time later. We were on the same program at Convention Hall in Philadelphia and the following morning before we headed our separate ways, he told me he had been talking to some RCA people about putting me under contract.

"You aren't under contract with anyone else, are you?"

"No. I do have a couple of records which are distributed by the Singspiration people, but I'm not under contract."

A few weeks later I was though, and, in the spring of 1951, I recorded *Inspiration Songs*. "It Is No Secret" was included because I liked it so much and because I wanted to say thanks to Stuart. Also on that album were "Ivory Palaces," "Known Only to Him," "Tenderly He Watches" and "If You Know the Lord," by Bickley Reichner which I got to introduce.

> If you know the Lord,
> You need nobody else,
> To see you through the darkest night.
> You can walk alone,
> You only need the Lord,
> He'll keep you on the road marked right.

I'll never forget that first recording session. The famous Hugo Winterhalter Orchestra provided the accompaniment and I was so nervous I couldn't do anything right. Finally, Steve Sholes got me on track and I managed to get the album recorded. It proved to be a very successful one, still being distributed. The RCA people called the album, No. 1187, "Old Faithful," and they continue to make it available.

It wasn't long before "Club Time" rang down the curtain on seven years of programs. A short time later, I finished eight years on "Songs in the Night." Providentially, I believe, that work was ended to make way for the adventure ahead with the Billy Graham Evangelistic Association. Soon came the "Hour of Decision" radio broadcasts, evenings of sacred concerts, Crusade work all over the world and a ministry through records.

It still seems like a dream.

4

Around the World with Song

The excitement that encompassed people who were a part of the Billy Graham team in those early years is hard to capture in words. So many dramatic things happened.

How the "Hour of Decision" came into being in 1950 has been told so often it doesn't need repeating. Enough to say, that the manner in which people responded with financial help to assure the program's first thirteen weeks on ABC was nothing short of miraculous.

I'll never forget the first program carried over 150 stations. We were holding a Crusade in Atlanta and we did the first show live. What electricity filled the air! Cliff emceed and led the singing. Jerry Beavan read the Crusade news report, which featured some of the exciting events happening. Grady read Scripture. I sang "I'd Rather Have Jesus" and Billy gave a stirring message.

Then, we sat back to await the verdict.

There were skeptics who thought the program would fail.

Others thought it would be just so-so, reaching the already churched, missing the unsaved, but approval of the program was not long coming. In five weeks, it had the largest audience of any religious program in history—reaching more people, some speculated, in a single night than D. L. Moody had spoken to in his lifetime.

Billy's spirit-filled and spirit-directed sermons are the life-blood of the program, of course, but music has also played a significant role. Cliff's part in selecting music, directing choirs, and producing the Hour of Decision have been crucial to its success. I have been privileged to be a part of the musical team, and have been blessed immeasurably.

The mail I've received from listeners of the Hour of Decision has been so gratifying — not because I have been a singer on the program but because there is great power in song messages. Dr. William Pentecost was not the first to recognize the efficacy of song but he made a poignant observation:

"I am profoundly sure," he wrote, "that among the ordained instrumentalists for the conversion and sanctification of the soul, God has not given a greater one, beside the preaching of the Gospel, than the singing of psalms and hymns and spiritual songs." Dwight L. Moody was as enthusiastic about the "singing of the gospel" and was one of the first to recognize the ability of spiritual music to reach men's hearts — even though he could not carry a tune himself.

In one of the more humorous stories in George Stebbins's book, he writes about Mr. Moody's problem:

I first thought [the discordant sound] was caused by something wrong with the organ . . . I listened to see if there might be one of the notes sounding when it ought to be silent, and found the discords were not from that source.

I was not long in doubt, however, for I soon heard the voice of Mr. Moody singing away as heartily as you please with no more idea of tune or time than a child. I then learned for the first time that he was one of the unfortunates who have no sense of pitch or harmony, and hence unable to recognize one tune from another . . . in spite of that defect, he . . . loved the sound of music and I have seen him . . . bowed under the power of an impressive hymn as I have known no other to be.

I would not be one to tell tales out of school, but a well-known evangelist friend of mine with whom I've been associated over twenty-five years has been afflicted with Mr. Moody's problem — the malady of no melody. This friend has a beautifully sonorous speaking voice and most would imagine an equally good singing voice, but it is not the case. Nonetheless, like Mr. Moody, he appreciates the power of a gospel song and he, too, joins in heartily.

My mail tells me time and again of the people who have been touched by gospel music. Seldom does a batch of letters fail to include a note from someone who has been helped through a serious problem by the message of a spiritual song.

From Australia comes a letter from a woman contemplating suicide who was dissuaded when she heard "I'd Rather Have Jesus" on the Hour of Decision. From Colorado, a letter from a man who heard a selection from a recent album over radio. The song, "He Will Hold Me Fast," gave him reassurance to face the future without his wife who had died of cancer. From California, a young housewife wrote me recently:

> I cannot afford a record player or records, but I hear you sing often over my little radio. Thank God for your ministry of song. Music has a way of lifting my spirits, especially gospel music. I heard you sing once at a nearby church and at that time you told us about your mother's favorite song, "Singing I Go." It has become my theme song. As you told us through song that night, "Jesus has lifted my load." Since then, I sing it whenever I'm feeling low and you were right, He does lift my load.

A woman from the South wrote me last January:

> For Christmas I received one of your records, but as my husband was very ill, I didn't play it. After his death and funeral a few weeks later, I came home to an empty house and for want of some sound to fill the void, I put your record on the phonograph. The first words I heard were, 'I know not what the future holds, but I know who

holds the future.' It was all I needed. I turned off the music. Divine strength swept over me and *light* came to me. It was a miracle how I went through that day. Thank God for the hymns of faith.

From a woman in the Midwest who attended one of our evenings of sacred songs.

Thank you, your pianist and your organization for bringing us a great sermon in song. A friend of my husband's who had lost all interest in the church came along to the program to please his wife. He was so moved he said he plans to begin attending church again.

Last week a letter from Maine came from a woman who had just received news her mother was dying in a distant state.

I couldn't go home and was heartbroken. My husband, on his way home from work, had the car radio on and he heard you singing a wonderful song called "Tenderly He Watches." He knew the words were just the ones I needed to hear so he drove several miles to get the record for me. I played it over and over and it sustained me through this difficult time. How great it is to know that through any ordeal, tenderly He watches over us.

Probably the most heartening letter I have received recently came from a young mother who lives behind the Iron Curtain. Her son is a voice student and wanted to sing gospel music, but they wrote me that none was available in their country. I sent a couple of records that got through. When the boy told his teacher that he wanted to sing gospel music, she didn't know what he meant. The mother wrote:

Then, God gives to Eddie's mind to ask her if she has gramaphone, he will bring her some records that she can know which kind of songs he wish to learn. She knows English and German language. When she heard this records, she was so happy she was playing all day during nearly one month. They liked "The Love of God" so much they translated it and then are singing so loud that the windows was trembling. Can you imagine what great courage

63

she has singing this Christians songs by opened window? Her house is on main street and everyone who passes hear the beautiful song. Eddie says she was jumping on her chair from happiness, playing piano and singing, telling: wonderful, wonderful.

I include these letter excerpts not because they reflect kindly on the singer, but that they testify again to the timeless power of gospel music and hymns to reach people and change lives.

Through recordings and radio programs such as the "Hour of Decision" our songs were soon reaching the far corners of the earth, and as the Crusade work grew I was privileged to visit many of these places in person.

One of our early trips was to England in 1949. It was on this trip that I learned the story behind Ira D. Sankey's "The Ninety and Nine," and though I have heard it told many times since, I had never read Sankey's account of it until Fred Bauer and I began to work on this book. In his book *Sankey's Story of the Gospel Hymns,* published in 1906 by the Philadelphia-based Sunday School Times Company, he wrote:

It was in the year 1874 that the poem, "The Ninety and Nine," was discovered, set to music, and sent out upon its world-wide mission. Its discovery seemed as if by chance, but I cannot regard it otherwise than providential. Mr. Moody had just been conducting a series of meetings in Glasgow, and I had been assisting him in his work as director of the singing. We were at the railway station at Glasgow and about to take the train for Edinburgh, whither we were going upon an urgent invitation of ministers to hold three days of meetings there before going into the Highlands. We had held a three months' series in Edinburgh just previous to our four months' campaign in Glasgow. As we were about to board the train I bought a weekly newspaper, for a penny. Being much fatigued by our incessant labors at Glasgow, and intending to begin work immediately upon our arrival at Edinburgh, we did not travel second- or third-class, as was our custom, but sought the seclusion and rest which a first-class railway carriage in Great Britain affords. In the hope of finding news from America I began perusing my lately purchased newspaper. This hope, however, was doomed to disappointment, as the only thing in its columns to remind an American of home and native land was a sermon by Henry Ward Beecher.

I threw the paper down, but shortly before arriving in Edinburgh I picked it up again with a view to reading the advertisements. While thus engaged my eyes fell upon a little piece of poetry in a corner of the paper. I carefully read it over, and at once made up my mind that this would make a great hymn for evangelistic work — if it had a tune. So impressed was I that I called Mr. Moody's attention to it, and he asked me to read it to him. This I proceeded to do with all the vim and energy at my command. After I had finished I looked at my friend Moody to see what the effect had been, only to discover that he had not heard a word, so absorbed was he in a letter which he had received from Chicago. My chagrin can be better imagined than described. Notwithstanding this experience, I cut out the poem and placed it in my musical scrap book — which, by the way, has been the seedplot from which sprang many of the Gospel songs that are now known throughout the world.

At the noon meeting on the second day, held at the Free Assembly Hall, the subject presented by Mr. Moody and other speakers was "The Good Shepherd." When Mr. Moody had finished speaking he called upon Dr. Bonar to say a few words. He spoke only a few minutes, but with great power, thrilling the immense audience by his fervid eloquence. At the conclusion of Dr. Bonar's words Mr. Moody turned to me with the question, "Have you a solo appropriate for this subject, with which to close the service?" I had nothing suitable in mind, and was greatly troubled to know what to do. The Twenty-third Psalm occurred to me, but this had been sung several times in the meeting. I knew that every Scotsman in the audience would join me if I sang that, so I could not possibly render this favorite psalm as a solo. At this moment I seemed to hear a voice saying: "Sing the hymn you found on the train!" But I thought this impossible, as no music had ever been written for that hymn. Again the impression came strongly upon me that I must sing the beautiful and appropriate words I had found the day before, and placing the little newspaper slip on the organ in front of me, I lifted my heart in prayer, asking God to help me so to sing that the people might hear and understand. Laying my hands upon the organ I struck the key of A flat, and began to sing.

Note by note the tune was given, which has not been changed from that day to this. As the singing ceased a great sigh seemed to go up from the meeting, and I knew that the song had reached the hearts of my Scots audience. Mr. Moody was greatly moved. Leaving the pulpit, he came down to where I was seated. Leaning over the organ, he looked at the little newspaper slip from which the song had been sung, and with tears in his eyes said: "Sankey, where did you get that hymn? I never heard the like of it in my life." I was also moved to tears and arose and replied: "Mr. Moody, that's the hymn I read to you yesterday on the train, which you did not hear." Then Mr. Moody raised his hand and pronounced the benediction, and the meeting closed. Thus "The Ninety and Nine" was born.

While visiting a mission (Carrubbers Close Mission in Edinburgh) Cliff Barrows and I were taken into a building and shown the very reed organ on which Sankey had composed the music for Elizabeth C. Clephane's poem. Invited to play it (the Scots call it a "Kist o' whustles") I picked out "The Ninety and Nine" from memory. It was a moving experience.

A few years later the mission gave the organ to the Billy Graham Evangelistic Association and it is now kept in the chapel of our headquarters building in Minneapolis. One time while I was visiting there, I participated in a service and sang "The Ninety and Nine" accompanying myself with that famous instrument. If you ever visit the BGEA offices in Minneapolis, be sure to look for Sankey's little organ. It will soon be 100 years since he first played that classic on it.

Mr. Sankey's book, which was written in 1906—two years before he died—contains so much interesting hymn nostalgia. In addition to stories behind the writing of many all-time gospel songs written by friends and acquaintances, Sankey talks about the origin of some of his own compositions, such as "I Am Praying for You," "Faith Is the Victory," "Jesus, I Will Trust Thee," "Hiding in Thee," and "There'll Be No Dark Valley."

He also talks about his long singing ministry in the company of Dwight L. Moody. In particular, I was moved in reading about his recollection of Mr. Moody's invitation to Sankey to join him, Sankey's hesitation, Moody's prayerful insistence, the vocalist's capitulation. He also talks about the many campaigns in which he shared the platform with the famed evangelist. In one passage, he relates that when Mr. Moody went on his second speaking trip to England in 1872, he (Sankey) was left in charge of the Tabernacle (in Chicago) "assisted by Major Whittle, Richard Thain, Fleming H. Revell and others." Mr. Revell was the founder of the company which originally published this book. He began the Fleming H. Revell Company in 1870 by publishing a collection of Moody's Sermons.

There are many anecdotes of fascination in the book, but no story is quite so steeped in history than his account of the Chicago Fire, Sunday, October 8, 1871. According to Sankey, he was participating with Moody in services at Farwell Hall and on this Sunday night, Mr. Moody had just finished his sermon and had asked Sankey to sing "Today the Saviour Calls." Sankey had reached the third verse of that hymn . . .

> Today the Saviour calls:
> For refuge fly;
> The storm of justice falls,
> And death is nigh . . .

when he reports "my voice was drowned by the loud noise of fire engines rushing past the hall and the tolling of bells." Mr. Moody immediately dismissed the congregation and all went out into the streets. Moody and Sankey stood for a moment looking at the ominous glow, then they separated—Sankey going across the river in the direction of the fire to offer his assistance, and Moody to his family on the north side. It was the last time they were to see each other for two months.

Sankey reports that the rapidly progressing fire soon drove him back across the river to Farwell Hall, which was soon to be consumed by fire. He gathered some of his most important possessions together in suitcases and tried to move them a half a mile's distance to Lake Michigan, but could find no transportation available so made two trips. Along the way, he assisted others to the water's edge and urged many people out of their apartments. He recalled that some "laughed me to scorn." Eventually, he took refuge in a boat until the fire had burned itself out. Then, he made his way home to his family in Pennsylvania by rail. It was several days before he learned by wire that Moody and his family also had escaped the flames.

It was on another trip to England for our London Crusade at Harringay Arena in 1954 that I came upon a newly translated hymn which was to become one of the favorites of our day— "How Great Thou Art." Though I didn't know the background then, I was to learn later the history of the song from its translater, S. K. Hine, an English missionary. The circuitous route it traveled to fame is most fascinating. Born in Sweden (and christened "O Great God") in 1885 at the hand of a preacher and editor named Carl Boberg, it was translated into German (by a man named Manfred von Glehn of Estonia) in 1907. Then, it went into Russian (translated by the Martin Luther of that country, Ivan S. Prokhanoff) in 1912. "How Great Thou Art" was put into English in 1925, but under the title "O Mighty God." Finally, in 1948, another translation was made from the Russian to the English (this time by Mr. Hine) and that version was entitled "How Great Thou Art." Mr. Hine included it in a magazine he published and people around the world wrote for copies. He obligingly made reprints and it was one of those copies that I was handed in 1954.

The poll in the front of this book showing it to be fourth on the all-time favorite list is not surprising to me. It is deserving of its esteem because jt uplifts all who hear it.

In the days since, it has become one of my most requested hymns along with "I'd Rather Have Jesus." During the 1957 New York Crusade I sang it over a hundred times. I also have recorded it three times for RCA and it has been used scores of times on the "Hour of·Decision."

England figures in the story behind a hymn I wrote in 1955, "The Wonder of It All." I was on my way to Scotland for meet-

How Great Thou Art

ings there aboard the S.S. *United States* bound for Southampton when inspiration came from conversation with another passenger. He wanted to know what went on at our meetings and after detailing the sequence of things at a typical Billy Graham Crusade meeting, I found myself at a loss for words when I tried to describe the response that usually accompanied Mr. Graham's invitation to become a Christian. "What happens then never becomes commonplace . . . watching people by the hundreds come forward . . . oh, if you could just see the wonder of it all."

"I think I should," he answered. Then, he wrote these words on a card and handed it back to me: THE WONDER OF IT ALL.

"That sounds like a song to me." Later that night, I wrote words on that theme and roughed out a melody to go with them. Since then, I've recorded "The Wonder of It All" and am happy to say that many other vocalists have recorded it, too.

I didn't think a great deal of it at first. For one thing I couldn't get one section to rhyme. That night on ship I wrote:

> **The wonder of sunset at evening,**
> **The wonder of sunrise at morn,**
> **But the wonder of wonders that thrills my soul,**
> **Is the wonder that God loves me.**

In Minneapolis a few months later for an engagement at the First Baptist Church, I told my friend Dr. Curtis B. Akenson about the experience and he encouraged me to sing it. I was reluctant and told the congregation so.

"Some of it doesn't rhyme."

It didn't matter apparently, because they responded enthusiastically to it and a few days later I called Cindy Walker, a dear friend from Texas, whose song-writing talent has put her name among the greats of today — both in religious and pop music. When I told her about my problem, she had a solution inside of a minute.

"How about this, Bev?" she advised.

> The wonder of sunset at evening,
> The wonder of sunrise *I see*,
> But the wonder of wonders that thrills my soul
> Is the wonder that God loves me.

And that's how it was published, thanks to a real songwriter, Cindy Walker!

After I had recorded it, Joe Blinco, a Britisher who was an associate evangelist on the Billy Graham team for many years, told me it was one of the most meaningful hymns he'd ever heard. I thanked him, thinking he was showing characteristic kindness, but I learned differently. Near the end of his life, he became the director of Forest Home in the High Sierras. It is a spiritual center established by the late Dr. Henrietta Mears for the young people of the Hollywood Presbyterian Church.

When Joe died, many of us went there for his funeral and I was pleased to have a part in honoring this great servant of God's. On my way into the chapel, I passed a tree that had been planted for him. On a bronze plaque at its base were these words: JOE BLINCO — THE WONDER OF IT ALL.

Travel is said to be broadening. It also has figured in the writing of many hymns. People on trips — planes, trains, ships; in strange places — have often been inspired to write.

I have had a couple of hymn writing experiences that happened while I was "on the road." In 1968 while participating in services in Australia, I was feeling rather blue one night, lonesome for family and home. Picking up my Bible which I always carry in my suitcase I turned to John and read:

> *Peace I leave with you, my peace I give unto you; not as the world giveth, give I unto you. Let not your heart be troubled, neither let it be afraid.* (John 14:27)

As I read, music came to me. I was reassured and uplifted. Taking a pencil in hand, I wrote notes around these words:

Let not your heart be troubled,
Neither let it be afraid,
My peace I leave with you,
My peace I leave with you,
Not as the world giveth,
Not as the world giveth,
My peace I leave with you.

Arthur Smith of Charlotte, North Carolina, took it from there. On a visit with him a short time later, he worked from my refrain, wrote verses for it, added a melody to his words and "Let Not Your Heart Be Troubled" was the result. I believe it was on that same visit that Arthur showed me a wonderful new composition of his which I have since recorded. Taking out his guitar (you may remember a pop tune called "Guitar Boogie" — well, he wrote it), he played and sang:

Acres of diamonds, mountains of gold,
Rivers of silver, jewels untold;
All these together, wouldn't buy you or me
Peace when we're sleeping or a conscience that's free.
A heart that's contented, a satisfied mind,
These are the treasures, money can't buy;
If you have Jesus, there's more wealth in your soul,
Than acres of diamonds, mountains of gold.

Though the words came to me unsolicited and I wrote the music at home, the hymn "Blue Galilee" resulted in a travel experience recently. Erma and I visited the Holy Land in the spring of 1971 with a group of eighty-nine people led by Roy Gustafson, a most knowledgeable guide and Bible scholar. It was such a wonderful experience visiting the significant places mentioned in the Scriptures.

One afternoon during the trip, we boarded a ship to travel from Tiberias to a kibbutz across the Sea of Galilee. By previous arrangement, a cassette recording of "Blue Galilee" was taken on board for playing. Midway across, the ship's captain shut down the engines and that recording I'd made some time before came over the ship's loudspeakers.

72

Roy said, "Maybe we can get Bev to sing along with it." And I did.

I will not soon forget the picture of our ship drifting through that beautiful sea. Later, the captain (M. A. Ezekiel) told me he would like a copy of the recording.

"It's so appropriate," he said. "I'd like to play it for all my passengers in the future."

· Maybe it is the change of scenery which inspires music. While Fred Bauer and I were working on this book, I was fiddling with the lyrics to a song which had been going through my head, but hadn't quite jelled. Then, Fred went with me to open the Shea summer cabin in Quebec (there's no phone there and we figured we could get in a couple of uninterrupted days on the manuscript). In that beautiful setting, I began revising the words to a song I've named "I Will Praise Him." I'm still not satisfied with it, but if it comes to anything that retreat will have figured in the result. (It is included in a recent album entitled "I'd Rather Have Jesus.") We used to go to a lake west of Ottawa as the guests of the Hibbert Vipond family. The Viponds are old friends of my family. Then, one summer, Hibbert said, "Bev, why not build a place here. I've got just the spot for you." He showed me a little island in a cove not far from his home on the water. "It's yours if you want it," he said. Erma and I were overjoyed.

It was characteristic generosity (his son and daughter-in-law, Denzil and Joy, are themselves just as giving). Anyway, we put up a small prefab, and the cabin has given the Shea family some wonderful memories.

Sometimes in traveling around the world, language becomes a barrier, and because I'm still trying to master English, I haven't had much success with some of the others. I remember a trip we made through Europe in 1955, visiting several different countries. In preparation for the tour, I attempted to learn at least one song in the language of each country on our itinerary. For example, I learned—phonetically—"Pass Me Not, O Gentle Saviour" in German, "He the Pearly Gates Will Open" in Swedish and "I'd Rather Have Jesus" in Finnish. Though I'm sure

The lead vocal sheet for the recording of "Blue Galilee." Arrangement by Bill Walker for the album *Whispering Hope*. Copyright 1947 by

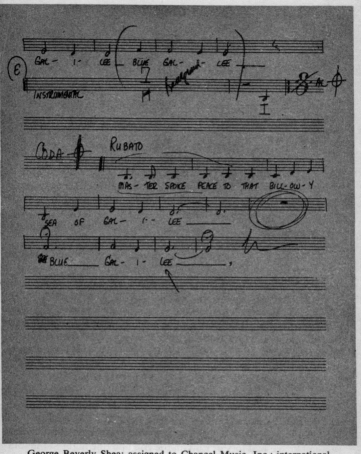

my accent and pronunciation left something to be desired, in each case, the audiences seemed to appreciate the attempts.

But the most vivid memory is our sailing out of Helsinki, Finland, following our meeting there. Many of the committee which had labored so hard to insure the visit a success came to the ship to see us off.

From the pier they called up to me, "Sing 'I'd Rather Have Jesus' again in our tongue." Fortunately, I had the phonetic version in my pocket. Handing it to Tedd Smith, he held the paper while I cupped my hands and sang. It was a meaningful way for me to say "goodbye" to some wonderful friends.

Not all my attempts with another tongue proved as successful, however. I tried to do "The Love of God" in French in Paris at Villedrôme d'hiver, but flubbed up despite David Barnes' coaching. The next day, Cliff—ever the diplomat—said, "You know Bev, I understand that here in France the man on the street knows many of the spirituals in English. I think you could do the spirituals here in English and get them across."

"Cliff, my friend," I told him, "I know what you are trying to say, and I agree with you, buddy." When I was growing up in Canada I heard a lot of beautiful French spoken—but not by me.

On this same trip, we visited many U.S. service installations and a documentary film entitled *Battleground Europe* was shot. I noted that the cameramen were around shooting footage each time I sang one of my translations. I thought that would provide some interesting sequences, but when the documentary came out, none of the "language" numbers were included. For my solo in the film, they used "Roll, Jordan, Roll." C'est la vie!

Another time, World Wide Pictures—which has produced such films as *Oil Town U.S.A., The Restless Ones, Two A Penny, Mr. Texas, Souls in Conflict* and *His Land* in addition to several documentaries—was filming a Crusade through Alabama. I remember we had lots of rain on the trip and one night in the football stadium at the University of Alabama, a terrible storm descended. To keep us dry on the platform, they covered us with a ghostly looking plastic, which kept whipping eerily in the wind.

Not content with that, our beloved Grady Wilson sat under an umbrella, which proved unwise. It pierced the plastic and was a target for the next bolt of lightning. Grady, though unhurt, was one of the first off the platform when the state police suggested we'd better "move out."

The crowd all gathered under the stands, and while waiting out the rain, Cliff conducted an informal song service. Someone called, "Bev, sing 'The Old Rugged Cross.' " I answered, "I will if you all hum along." And so we began.

While I was singing I noticed the World Wide cameramen shooting the scene, hundreds of people huddled together as if in the catacombs singing "The Old Rugged Cross."

Afterward, Frank Jacobson, producer of the documentary commented; "I hope we got this on film. It was very moving."

I looked forward to seeing it on the documentary. But it was left on the cutting room floor, too. My song in the film was again "Roll, Jordan, Roll." Just call me Johnny One Note.

In the course of my travels, its been my pleasant duty to sing before the president of the United States—twice each before Presidents Eisenhower, Johnson and Nixon. Twice the event was the Presidential Prayer Breakfast in Washington.

The first time was impromptu in 1954, when I was asked to lead those gathered in one of my favorites:

> **What a friend we have in Jesus**
> **All our sins and griefs to bear!**
> **What a privilege to carry**
> **Everything to God in prayer!**
>
> *Oh, what peace we often forfeit*
> *Oh, what needless pain we bear,*
> *All because we do not carry,*
> *Everything to God in prayer!*

My surprise came the next morning when (dressed in an old bathrobe and slippers) I sat down to breakfast with Erma back home. As the TV in the kitchen came into focus whom should I see on the "Today Show" but old psalm singer Shea—singing his heart out. And on his right stood the president joining in. He knew the words, no question about that.

A few months later, I was invited to the National Christian Endeavor's annual convention in Washington. Though President Eisenhower was expected to put in an appearance and make a few brief remarks, I doubted he would be present when I sang. However, he lingered afterward and was on hand when I sang "I'd Rather Have Jesus." Before he left he shook my hand and said:

"Thank you for that song."

I was deeply touched.

The most recent experience in which I was privileged to sing before a president came in January, 1969, at the White House. Mr. Nixon had just been inaugurated and had invited Billy Graham to conduct the first Sunday religious service in the East Room. Billy asked T. W. Wilson (Grady's brother), Tedd Smith and me to go with him and take part in the service. I sang "How Great Thou Art" that day. And though the service was impressive, some of the events leading up to it remain more vivid in my memory. We went to the White House early that day to have breakfast with the president, Mrs. Nixon and their daughter, Tricia, in their private quarters. They were so warm and casual. Mrs. Nixon sat at my left, Tricia at my right. On around the table were Billy and Ruth Graham, Tedd, T. W. and the president.

The conversation was light and in a good-natured vein all through the meal. After breakfast, Mrs. Nixon showed us around the White House while Billy and the president went off to discuss the details of the service, but we regrouped with time to spare. While waiting for those invited to the service to arrive, the president went to a nearby grand piano and began playing—very well. But it was not his skill but his selection which took me by surprise. It was "He Will Hold Me Fast." As I stood nearby, I began humming.

"Do you know it?" he asked.

"Yes, I sang it as a boy."

I wondered where a man with Quaker roots had learned such an old-time hymn. Not long ago I think I got the answer: He learned the hymn at the Church of the Open Door in Los Angeles. When the president was a boy I understand he attended a series of services conducted there by the Reverend Paul Rader, whose theme song happened to be "He Will Hold Me Fast."

> When I fear my faith will fail,
> Christ will hold me fast:
> When the tempter would prevail,
> He can hold me fast.
>
> *He will hold me fast,*
> *For my Saviour loves me so,*
> *He will hold me fast.*

Not long after that I recorded it for RCA and when the liner copy (comments on the back about the album) was being prepared I was asked about the hymn. When I told the writer why I'd included it, he wanted to use the story, but I vetoed the idea, thinking it would be presumptuous to make such speculation without more substantiation. I include the story here only because I have space to explain that it is speculation.

(Incidentally, President Nixon was sent a copy of that album *These Are the Things that Matter* and he responded appreciatively.)

I am privy to many fascinating events thanks to Billy who graciously includes me often. For instance, I went with him to Plymouth, Massachusetts, in December, 1970, for the 350th anniversary of the Mayflower landing, and sang on the program. When I accepted the invitation, I was interested to see that Norman Clayton was to lead the choir. Our paths first crossed in 1943 when I was helping Jack Wyrtzen in New York. Norman was working for Thomas Bakeries, the English muffin people, then— writing gospel music in his spare time. It was Jack who encouraged him to publish some of his compositions and Norman put together a book from scratch—typesetting, printing, and binding. I hadn't seen him in some time, so I was anticipating the reunion. Norman, as many of you know, is an accomplished composer, who wrote one of my first-line favorites "If We Could See Beyond Today."

However, when I got to Plymouth the man who was conducting the music was not the one I expected. It was Norman, Jr. If that didn't make me look in the mirror for gray hairs! But like his father, he has wonderful musical talent and did a great job that day.

I sang two songs. One was entitled "O God, Beneath Thy Guiding Hand," a number I've had in my little black book for many years, and its lyrics were certainly appropriate. Unfortunately, the tune was not particularly strong, so I worked on a new one for the occasion.

> O God, beneath Thy guiding hand
> Our exiled fathers crossed the sea;
> And when they trod the wintry strand,
> With prayer and psalm they worshipped Thee.
>
> Thou heard'st (You heard) well-pleased, the song, the prayer;
> Thy blessing came, and still its power
> Shall onward through all ages, bear
> The memory of that holy hour.
>
> Laws, freedom, truth and faith in God
> Came with those exiles o'er the waves;
> And where their pilgrim feet have trod
> The God they trusted guards their graves (guarded their days)
>
> And here Thy name, O God of love,
> Their children's children shall adore,
> Till these eternal hills remove,
> And spring adorns the earth no more.

For the second selection, I chose "Take Time to Pray," a hymn recorded in 1952 on my second album. It also had words that fit. They hold a message for us all:

I've been going my way
Living life day by day
Never thinking or stopping to pray
Till the storm clouds came near
Taking loved ones so dear
Now I'm trying to live God's way.

Take time to pray,
Bow your head in prayer every day
Oh, please dear God, please keep us free
For you know what this land means to me
Take time to pray, never let me O Lord go astray
Though the world may look dark and my soul holdeth fear
Let me know, dear Lord, thou art near.

Special occasions require special attention be given to the selection of numbers, and I always try to give a great deal of prayer
to the choices. One of my most memorable Christmases was
spent in Vietnam in 1966. We were at An Khe for Christmas Eve,
caught in a rainstorm that didn't look as if it was going to stop in
time for the service, but it did and we had a wonderful meeting.
On that occasion I chose that old favorite composed by Longfellow, "I Heard the Bells on Christmas Day" . . .

> Then pealed the bells more loud and deep:
> "God is not dead, nor doth He sleep,
> The wrong shall fail, the right prevail
> With peace on earth, good will to men."

Of course, the standards at Christmas are always good choices.
That same service was closed by Cliff leading everyone in "Silent
Night." A Catholic chaplain had given each soldier a paper cup
with a candle in it and just before we sang that blessed Christmas
hymn, we all lit our candles. It was a beautiful sight.

The story behind "Silent Night" has always been one of my
favorites, and though I have seen many tellings of it, none is
more beautiful than one I read in *Guideposts* magazine's annual
Christmas booklet several years ago. Glenn D. Kittler told it
like this:

Sadly the young pastor strolled through the snow-covered slopes above the village of Oberndorf, Austria. In a few days it would be Christmas Eve, but Josef Mohr knew there would be no music in his church to herald the great event. The new organ had broken down.

Pausing, Pastor Mohr gazed at the scattered lights in the village below. The sight of the peaceful town, huddled warmly in the foothills, stirred his imagination. Surely it was on such a clear and quiet night as this that hosts of angels sang out the glorious news that the Saviour had been born.

The young cleric sighed heavily as he thought, "If only we here in Oberndorf could celebrate the birth of Jesus with glorious music like the shepherds heard on that wonderful night."

Standing there, his mind filled with visions of the first Christmas, Josef Mohr suddenly became aware that disappointment was fading from his heart; in its place surged a great joy. Vividly, he saw the manger, carved from a mountain side; he saw Mary and Joseph and the Child; he saw the strangers who had been attracted by the light of the great star. The image seemed to shape itself into the words of a poem.

The next day he showed the poem to Franz Gruber, the church organist, who said, "These words should be sung at Christmas. But what could we use for accompaniment? This?" Glumly, he held up his guitar.

The pastor replied, "Like Mary and Joseph in the stable, we must be content with what God provides for us."

Franz Gruber studied the poem, then softly strummed the melody that came to him. Next he put the words to the melody and sang them. When he finished, his soul was ablaze with its beauty.

On Christmas Eve, 1818, in a small Austrian village, the Oberndorf choir, accompanied only by a guitar, sang for the first time the immortal hymn that begins, "Silent Night, . . . Holy Night."

I remember another moving experience that Christmas — hearing Anita Bryant's rendition of "The Battle Hymn of the Republic" sung before an audience of 10,000 soldiers. Bob Hope's show had gotten its usual roaring reception. It had the expected number of beautiful girls clad in the expectedly stunning costumes. They sang and danced to the expected chorus of cheers and wolf whistles. But none of their applause matched that they gave to Anita when she concluded the program with that great Civil War hymn. I have seldom heard anything to rival their response. Deafening. And no one performs it as dramatically as Anita.

Like other majestic hymns in that category ("How Great Thou Art," "You'll Never Walk Alone," and the like) it has lyrics that bring goose pimples to the spine. It was written in 1861 by Julia Ward Howe, a dedicated Christian teacher of blind children in New York City and a friend of President Lincoln. Early in the Civil War, he invited Mrs. Howe, a noted reformer, to join a group of people he was taking on a visit to the sight of a recent battle. Mrs. Howe accepted the invitation. On the trip, she heard many Union soldiers singing around the campfire, but one song moved her deeply. It was about John Brown, the slavery abolitionist who was hanged for his part in the famous Harpers Ferry raid. When Mrs. Howe returned to Washington, she couldn't get the tune she had heard out of her mind and its haunting melody stirred her to compose new words for it—words which reflected her faith in those trying days. In a Washington hotel room, she wrote the hymn which was to become the marching song of an Army and in years to come a testimony of faith for a nation.

Mine eyes have seen the glory of the coming of the Lord;
He is trampling out the vintage where the grapes of wrath are stored;
He hath loosed the fateful lightning of His terrible swift sword;
His truth is marching on.

Glory! glory, hallelujah!
Glory! glory, hallelujah!
Glory! glory, hallelujah!
Our God is marching on.

Easter is another one of those special occasions which calls for prayerful song selection. One of my favorite Easter solos is "Were You There?" and I've sung it in some memorable sunrise services — at Soldier Field in Chicago and in the Rose Bowl, each before audiences in the tens of thousands.

But the time I cherish most is just before this last Easter when I was in Jerusalem at the Garden Tomb in the Gordon's Calvary area. The keeper of the tomb, a young man who was converted at our Amsterdam Crusade a few years ago, asked me to sing "Were You There?" for the group touring that historic site. I did as he asked concluding with a different ending from that which was written.

Though not original with me, I think the last stanza should be more triumphant than that in the books. So instead of singing:

Were you there when they laid him in the tomb?

I sing:

> **Were you there when He rose up from the dead?**
> **Were you there when He rose up from the dead?**
> **Sometimes I feel like shouting "Glory, glory, glory."**
> **Were you there when He rose up from the dead?**

That sentiment more accurately states my feelings about Christ's victory over death.

Songs That Lift the Heart

A few years ago I did an album entitled *Hymns That Have Lived 100 Years*. It included such numbers as "Rock of Ages," "Fairest Lord Jesus," "Nearer My God To Thee," and "Abide With Me." Of course, many hymns we sing today are over 100 years old. Age neither dims their truth or beauty nor does it lessen the impact of some of the legends that have followed these hymns through their decades of popularity.

Singing "Jesus, Lover of My Soul" recently I was reminded of a story Ira D. Sankey told about that Charles Wesley composition. One afternoon on a Hudson River liner out of New York, Sankey was singing that song to a gathering of people.

> **Jesus, lover of my soul,**
> **Let me to Thy bosom fly . . .**

When a man came to him excitedly out of the crowd. "Were you in the Union Army?" the man asked.

"Yes, I served in Maryland."

"Were you at such and such battle?"

"Yes."

"Could you have been singing that hymn one night while you were on sentry duty?"

"Yes, I even remember the night," Sankey told him.

"And I remember having a bead on you, but hearing you sing that great hymn I could not squeeze the trigger."

That story has a World War II parallel. It is told by a friend of mine, Burt Frizen, who lives in Wheaton, Illinois. While attending college at Wheaton, Burt distinguished himself with his fine baritone voice. But his college studies were interrupted by the war. Serving in Germany, he was seriously wounded and lay dying for six hours. He passed in and out of consciousness, aware at each wakening that his life was ebbing faster and faster.

To face that moment, he began singing a hymn his mother had taught him.

> There is a name to me so dear,
> Like sweetest music to my ear;
> For when my heart is troubled, filled with fear,
> Jesus whispers peace.

As he sang, a German soldier came upon him, his bayonet fixed. Burt anticipated the worst but kept singing. As he sang he felt himself being lifted up. He was carried to a nearby stone ledge. There the enemy soldier left Burt unharmed. A few minutes later, he was discovered and rescued by his own medics.

Though the great hymns of the past are fine, they should not cloud our perception to recognize that some inspiring music is being written today. As I try to select contemporary numbers to sing, I often wonder which of them will be in hymn books a hundred years from now. More than a few, I suspect.

It has been my privilege to know many of the leading hymn writers and gospel musical talents of our day and they are truly an outstanding lot—well-schooled, dedicated, committed—such men as John Peterson of Grand Rapids, musical editor of the Singspiration series, published by Zondervan. One of the most prolific composers today, John does both words and music—and does them well. How many times have you sung:

> It took a miracle to put the stars in place
> It took a miracle to hang the world in space
> But when He saved my soul, cleansed, and made me whole,
> It took a miracle of love and grace.

Many times, right? Well, then you know John Peterson by music and poetry if not by face. He also has written "Shepherd of Love" and a beautiful Christmas cantata.

I first came into contact with John when he joined the staff of WMBI in the mid forties. Few people who ever heard his sign-off program at sundown will ever forget it. (WMBI's license limits its broadcasting hours to sunset so John's program closed the day for the station.) Playing an Hawaiian guitar, his tender interpretation of the old hymns could and did bring tears to the eyes. As a matter of fact, the station still plays those tapes and his music still has the same effect on me. He was often accompanied at the organ by some other dear friends of mine — Don Hustad, John Innes and Gil Mead. All of them deserve the appreciation of gospel music lovers for the dedication of their talents to the Lord.

Gil and John live nearby and are available when I need help. Not long ago, Gil played for me in Oklahoma City at a state teachers' convention and afterward we got to talking about his hobby — building and repairing pipe organs.

"Do you ever have any pipes you don't know what to do with?" I asked him.

"Do I," he said. "Come over and I'll give you a barrelfull."

And that's just what happened. I must have transferred a hundred pipes from Gil's basement to mine. I don't know what I'm going to do with them, except maybe blow a high E once in a while. (Whenever I let go with one of those blasts from the basement, I always give Erma a start. "Boys must play," she will call down from the kitchen.)

Another dedicated Christian musician is John Innes from Scotland. He heard the Crusade from Harringay Arena in London over the old World War II telephone land lines which carried broadcasts to 500 auditoriums throughout the islands. That was a providential windfall. Had it not been for Bob Benninghoff, ABC engineer out of Chicago, John and millions of others would not have heard those services. Bob Benninghoff had remembered that during World War II land lines had been used to communicate throughout Great Britain. He contacted the post office department, found the lines to be intact and permission was received to use them during the Crusade.

John Innes was one of those who heard the broadcasts. He was a boy of sixteen then. At eighteen, he came to America. He graduated from Wheaton and received his Masters at Northwestern University.

It was during this time that the paths of Don Hustad and John Innes crossed. Speaking of Don, few people in this line of work are more respected than he is.

After many years with the Billy Graham team, he is now a full-time professor of music at Louisville's Southern Baptist Seminary. He still finds time to travel with me to an occasional evening of sacred music concert or to help out at a Crusade.

There are so many memories Don and I share about music from WMBI through some of the great Crusade meetings right up to the present. While I was working on this book, Don played at the Lexington, Kentucky, Crusade and then accompanied me on a series of concerts.

He reminds me of so many past highlights whenever we get together. For example, not long ago while playing the invitation hymn "Just As I Am" he put a tag on the end of it that sent my mind tumbling back a few years to the Copenhagen meetings. There, they sing "Just As I Am" the same as we do until the end. Then, after "I come, I come" they add "Oh, Lamb of God, I come." Whereas we usually end on what we call "a third," they close on the dominant of the chord. Now whenever Don wants to remind me of those wonderful meetings in Denmark, all he must do is use that leitmotif technique and he's got me.

Others on the Billy Graham musical team such as Tedd Smith and Cliff Barrows have had a great influence on gospel music in our time. Tedd's talent could have certainly carried him far in the classical field, or for that matter in any direction he chose. I'm thankful he was led into ministry of sacred music because he has been a great blessing to so many.

Recently, he composed a clever song in a modern idiom which has captivated audiences, both at home and abroad. Called "The

Running Man," it tells in ballad form the story of a man who ran scared all his life until he met Jesus. Finally, his running over, Tedd tells about the man's new peace as he plays "I Know That My Redeemer Liveth."

"The Running Man" draws praise whenever Tedd presents it. With the exception of Cliff and me, Tedd has been on the BGEA musical team longer than anyone, and his friendship and support have provided constant joy in my work.

Cliff's talents know no limit—neither does his enthusiasm for singing the gospel. He, probably more than anyone else, has helped relax me on the platform and I've always needed a little help in this department. No one can do his best if he's tense, and Cliff's sincerity, warmth, grace, and sense of humor have given the Crusades a wonderful informal flavor. I'll never forget the night in San Francisco's Cow Palace in front of a full house when I forgot the words to "Make the Courts of Heaven Ring." Tedd, who sometimes may not know what I'm going to sing until I go to the mike, was given the signal: two fingers down; meaning two flats, and I began:

> "Holy, holy" is what the angels sing,
> And I expect to help them
> Make the courts of heaven ring. . . .

All at once my mind went blank. Tedd began the second verse without me.

"Cliff," I said, turning around, "I guess you'll have to help. Mother told me this would happen someday, but I never figured it would happen at the Cow Palace."

The crowd broke into a big round of applause and I picked up the music at the chorus.

When it was over, Cliff had some funny line which brought another laugh and the service proceeded. One other thing: After that I started carrying a copy of the words in my little black book just in case!

Still, of all Cliff's talents, preaching, singing, song leading, acting (I thought he did a great job in the film *His Land* as did our friend Cliff Richard) his genius is no more in evidence than when he is rehearsing and honing a choir. Inside a few minutes, he can take thousands of strangers and blend their voices into a symphony of ear-pleasing and soul-stirring music. He's the Robert Shaw of our field — no question about it.

Speaking of the film *His Land* brings to mind the name of Ralph Carmichael again. He composed the musical score for this picture which includes the beautiful "The New 23rd," which I recorded recently. All told, Ralph has written in the neighborhood of seventy-five motion picture scores and he has done all the music for the BGEA's World Wide Picture productions. In addition, he has written a great many things for TV, and a list of great songs that make one wonder how he has time to sleep.

A contributor to both secular and sacred music, the California-based composer can swing from music for Roger Williams, the King Family, Jack Jones, or Peggy Lee to gospel music without missing a note. The son of a minister, Ralph admits to liking sacred music best and his writing in this category has thrilled millions. I've done several of his numbers, and all of them are what my old singing coach, Emerson Williams, would call "heart songs." Among Ralph's songs are: "He's Everything to Me," "All My Life" and "The Saviour Is Waiting." One of my favorites to come from Ralph's pen is "I Found What I Wanted." The words are only matched by the music for beauty:

> I found what I wanted
> When I found the Lord,
> I found more than pleasures
> Of earth could afford,
> I knew the moment I knelt
> How rich my life really could be,
> Yes, God did this for me.

I first worked with Ralph at a recording session in 1959 when he arranged and conducted the album, "The Love of God," but my friendship with him dates several years earlier than that when he was arranging and conducting for Christian films. There is always something distinctively original about anything Ralph touches. His music is lilting, happy, inspiring.

Another exciting composer today is Cindy Walker who can and does write both religious and popular music. I first met Cindy in 1951 during the Hollywood Crusade. We were invited out to the home of Y. P. Freeman, then vice-president of Paramount. Billy spoke to the guests, about sixty people as I recall, and he invited them to accept Christ. Several people made commitments and one of them was Cindy. Several days later she wrote what the experience meant to her:

> Oh, how sweet it is to know:
> Jesus loves me,
> That wherever I may go:
> Jesus loves me,
> In His love each day I'm growing,
> With the glory just of knowing
> Jesus loves me.
>
> On the cross in deep distress he set me free
> Greater love hath none than this:
> He died for me,
> So, oh, grave, where is thy power,
> He's my strength, my shining tower,
> Star of sorrow's darkest hour,
> Jesus loves me.

I've recorded that number along with many other of Cindy's, who has more than 400 copyrighted songs. Among her religious gems I like: "A Child of the King," "Tender Farewell," "O Gentle Shepherd" and "Beloved Enemy."

Her pop successes include: "You Don't Know Me," "In the Misty Moonlight," "Dream Baby," "Distant Drums."

A Texan who spends half her time in the Lone Star State and half the year in Nashville, she comes from a musical family. Her grandfather, F. L. Eiland, wrote "Hold to God's Unchanging Hand" and her mother, affectionately known as Mama to people in the recording business, is an accomplished pianist. But Cindy's story is a modern fairy tale. As a young girl of seventeen, living

91

in California, she hand-carried her first composition into the offices of Bing Crosby and handed it to him. It was entitled "Lone Star Trail." Bing liked it and used it in his next picture. Since then Eddy Arnold, Perry Como, Jim Reeves, Andy Williams, Glenn Campbell — the list goes on and on — have recorded Cindy Walker-written songs and with great results.

Of course, Cindy can and does sing occasionally. And she does it well.

Speaking of her vocal ability makes me aware that I have written a great deal about composers and gospel instrumentalists, but have said little about some of the talented people who sing the lyrics. If I get started, however, I don't know where I'll stop. In particular, I'd single out some of the people who have come forward to lend their talents during Crusades — Ethel Waters, Lawrence Welk star Norma Zimmer, Myrtle Hall of Greenville, South Carolina, Anita Bryant — I'm going to stop! There are many who could be named.

I cannot go on without telling you a personal experience my wife Erma and I had recently with Ethel Waters, our dear friend. As many know, she sings with us several times a year now, thrilling audiences with such great ones as "His Eye Is on the Sparrow" and "Oh, How I Love Jesus." Ethel is a sterling example of what I mean when I say, you can tell a person's commitment by the conviction in his voice. She means what she sings.

Many will recall, Ethel came to us during the 1957 Crusade in New York. One night she showed up and sang in the choir. The next night she came back and before that Crusade was over, she was giving her message in song to those vast crowds which packed Madison Square Garden.

Not long ago, she was in Chicago to star in the revival of the Broadway musical, "Member of the Wedding." As you can guess, she was a four-bell hit. Before returning to the Coast, she came out and spent her last night in our home. How we all enjoyed her visit.

After dinner, we sat and talked and I got to fiddling around at the piano. Ethel got to singing and I couldn't resist turning on my